T0274594

Multi-Engine Pilot

ORAL EXAM GUIDE

JASON BLAIR
Based on original text by Michael D. Hayes

NINTH EDITION

COMPREHENSIVE PREPARATION
FOR THE FAA CHECKRIDE

AVIATION SUPPLIES & ACADEMICS, INC.
NEWCASTLE, WASHINGTON

Multi-Engine Pilot Oral Exam Guide
Ninth Edition
by Jason Blair
based on original text by Michael D. Hayes

Aviation Supplies & Academics, Inc.
7005 132nd Place SE
Newcastle, Washington 98059
asa@asa2fly.com | 425-235-1500 | asa2fly.com

See the Reader Resources at **asa2fly.com/oegme** for additional information and updates relating to this book.

ASA-OEG-ME9
ISBN 978-1-64425-401-1

Additional formats available:
eBook EPUB ISBN 978-1-64425-402-8
eBook PDF   ISBN 978-1-64425-403-5

Printed in the United States of America
2027 2026 2025 2024   9 8 7 6 5 4 3 2 1

Library of Congress Cataloging-in-Publication Data:
Names: Blair, Jason, author. | Hayes, Michael D., author.
Title: Multi-engine pilot oral exam guide : comprehensive preparation for the FAA checkride / Jason Blair, based on original text by Michael D. Hayes.
Description: Ninth edition. | Newcastle, Washington : Aviation Supplies & Academics, Inc., 2024. | "ASA-OEG-ME9"—Title page verso.
Identifiers: LCCN 2024014534 (print) | LCCN 2024014535 (ebook) | ISBN 9781644254011 (trade paperback) | ISBN 9781644254028 (epub) | ISBN 9781644254035 (pdf)
Subjects: LCSH: United States. Federal Aviation Administration—Examinations—Study guides. | Multiengine flying—Examinations—Study guides. | Oral examinations—Study guides. | LCGFT: Study guides.
Classification: LCC TL711.T85 B58 2024 (print) | LCC TL711.T85 (ebook) | DDC 629.132/52076—dc23/eng/20240415
LC record available at https://lccn.loc.gov/2024014534
LC ebook record available at https://lccn.loc.gov/2024014535

Contents

About the Author

Jason Blair is an active single- and multi-engine instructor and an FAA Designated Pilot Examiner (DPE) with over 6,000 hours total time, over 3,500 hours of instruction given, and more than 3,500 hours in aircraft as a DPE. In his role as an Examiner, he has issued more than 2,500 pilot certificates. Blair has worked for and continues to work with multiple aviation associations with his work focusing on pilot training and testing. His experience as a pilot goes back over 30 years, as an instructor spans over 20 years, and includes more than 100 makes and models of aircraft flown. Blair has written and continues to write for multiple aviation publications with a focus on training and safety.

In addition to ASA's Oral Exam Guide series, Blair is also the author of four books in ASA's Aviator's Field Guide series: *Buying an Airplane, Owning an Airplane, Tailwheel Flying,* and *Middle-Altitude Flying.*

Introduction

The *Multi-Engine Pilot Oral Exam Guide* is a comprehensive guide designed for pilots training for the addition of a Multi-Engine Land Rating to an existing pilot certificate. This guide is equally valuable to students training under Part 61 or in a Part 141 flight school. It is also well paired with the *Private Pilot Oral Exam Guide* or *Commercial Pilot Oral Exam Guide*, depending on the certificate level the pilot is seeking while also flying a multi-engine aircraft. The guide also proves beneficial to pilots who wish to refresh their knowledge or who are preparing for a flight review.

This book is divided into four main sections. The first three chapters represent the basic knowledge areas that must be demonstrated by applicants before they are issued a Multi-Engine Rating. The fourth chapter is a general review of the Airman Certification Standards (ACS) tasks required during the flight portion of the checkride. You should review the ACS applicable to your particular certification in addition to the material in this section. For additional reference, several appendixes have been included at the end of this guide. Appendix 1 contains the "Applicant's Practical Test Checklist" to be used when making final preparations for the checkride. Appendix 2 contains questions common to understanding of aircraft performance, limitations, systems, and procedures that are particularly helpful when checking out in a new airplane. Appendix 3, "Operations of Aircraft Without/With an MEL," depicts the typical sequence of events a pilot, operating with or without an MEL, should follow when inoperative equipment is discovered to be on board. Appendix 4 is a copy of the FAA's "Light Twin Takeoff Control and Performance Briefing."

An FAA evaluator may ask questions at any time during the practical test to determine whether the applicant has the required knowledge. Based on intensive debriefings conducted after checkrides, we have provided you with the questions and topics commonly asked along with the information or the appropriate references necessary for a knowledgeable response.

You may supplement this guide with other comprehensive study materials as noted in brackets at the end of each answer; for example: [PA.I.G, CA.I.G; FAA-H-8083-25]. The first items provided are ACS codes for the relevant Areas of Operation and Tasks from the *Private Pilot for Airplane Category Airman Certification Standards* (FAA-S-ACS-6) and *Commercial Pilot for Airplane Category Airman Certification Standards* (FAA-S-ACS-7). Additional references pertaining to the questions can be found in the ACS listed under the Tasks corresponding to the provided ACS codes. The next reference(s) in the brackets are other study materials for which abbreviations and corresponding titles are listed below.

Be sure that you use the latest revision of these references when reviewing for the test. Also, check the ASA website at asa2fly.com/oegme for the most recent updates to this book due to changes in FAA procedures and regulations as well as for Reader Resources containing additional relevant information and updates.

14 CFR Part 23	*Airworthiness Standards: Normal Category Airplanes*
14 CFR Part 43	*Maintenance, Preventive Maintenance, Rebuilding, and Alteration*
14 CFR Part 45	*Identification and Registration Marking*
14 CFR Part 61	*Certification: Pilots, Flight Instructors, and Ground Instructors*
14 CFR Part 91	*General Operating and Flight Rules*
AC 61-67	*Stall and Spin Awareness Training*
AC 91-73	*Parts 91 and 135 Single-Pilot, Flight School Procedures During Taxi Operations*
AC 120-80	*Firefighting of General and High-Energy In-Flight Fires*
AC 150/5340-18	*Standards for Airport Sign Systems*
AFM	*FAA-Approved Airplane Flight Manual*
AIM	*Aeronautical Information Manual*
drs.faa.gov	*Dynamic Regulatory System—Order 8900.1*
FAA-H-8083-1	*Aircraft Weight and Balance Handbook*
FAA-H-8083-2	*Risk Management Handbook*
FAA-H-8083-3	*Airplane Flying Handbook*

FAA-H-8083-15	*Instrument Flying Handbook*
FAA-H-8083-16	*Instrument Procedures Handbook*
FAA-H-8083-25	*Pilot's Handbook of Aeronautical Knowledge*
FAA-H-8083-30	*Aviation Maintenance Technician Handbook—General*
FAA-H-8083-31	*Aviation Maintenance Technician Handbook—Airframe*
FAA-H-8083-32	*Aviation Maintenance Technician Handbook—Powerplant*
FAA-P-8740-2	*Density Altitude*
FAA-P-8740-13	*Engine Operation for Pilots*
FAA-P-8740-66	*Flying Light Twins Safely*
FAA-S-ACS-6	*Private Pilot for Airplane Category Airman Certification Standards*
FAA-S-ACS-7	*Commercial Pilot for Airplane Category Airman Certification Standards*
FAA-S-ACS-8	*Instrument Rating–Airplane Airman Certification Standards*
FAA Safety ALC-30	*FAA Multi-Engine Safety Review*
POH	*Pilot's Operating Handbook*
SAIB CE-05-51	*FAA Special Airworthiness Information Bulletin*
SAIB CE-10-11	*FAA Special Airworthiness Information Bulletin— Electrical: Fire Hazard in Resetting Circuit Breakers (C/Bs)*

Most of these documents are available on the FAA's website (faa.gov). Additionally, many of the publications are reprinted by ASA (asa2fly.com) and are available from aviation retailers worldwide.

A review of the appropriate ACS and the information presented in this guide should provide you with the necessary preparation for the FAA Multi-Engine Land practical test.

Multi-Engine
Operations   **1**

A. Required Documents/Airworthiness

1. What documents are required on board an aircraft prior to flight?

Supplements (14 CFR §91.9)

Placards (14 CFR §91.9)

Airworthiness Certificate (14 CFR §91.203)

Registration Certificate (14 CFR §91.203)

Radio Station License—if operating outside of U.S.; FCC regulation (47 CFR §87.18)

Operating limitations—AFM/POH and supplements, placards, markings (14 CFR §91.9)

Weight and balance data—current (14 CFR §23.2620)

Compass Deviation Card (14 CFR §23.1547)

External Data Plate/Serial Number (14 CFR §45.11)

Exam Tip: During the practical test, your evaluator may wish to examine the various required aircraft documents (SPARROW) during the preflight inspection, as well as the currency of any aeronautical charts, EFB data, etc., on board the aircraft. Prior to the test, verify that all of the necessary aircraft documentation, onboard databases, charts, etc., are current and available.

[PA.I.B, CA.I.B; 14 CFR 91.9, 91.203]

2. What are the required tests and inspections to be performed on multi-engine aircraft? (Include inspections for IFR.)

Annual inspection within the preceding 12 calendar months. (14 CFR §91.409)

Airworthiness directives (ADs) and life-limited parts complied with, as required. (14 CFR §§91.403, 91.417)

VOR equipment check every 30 days (for IFR ops). (14 CFR §91.171)

100-hour inspection, if used for hire or flight instruction in aircraft CFI provides. (14 CFR §91.409)

Altimeter, altitude reporting equipment, and static pressure systems tested and inspected (for IFR ops), every 24 calendar months. (14 CFR §91.411)

Transponder tests and inspections, every 24 calendar months. (14 CFR §91.413)

Emergency locator transmitter, operation and battery condition inspected every 12 calendar months. (14 CFR §91.207)

Exam Tip: Be prepared to locate all of the required inspections, ADs, life-limited parts, etc., in the aircraft and engine logbooks and be able to determine when the next inspections are due. Create an aircraft status sheet that indicates the status of all required inspections, ADs, life-limited parts, and other related items. Use post-it notes to tab the specific pages in the aircraft and engine logbooks.

[PA.I.B, CA.I.B; 14 CFR 91.171, 91.207, 91.409, 91.411, 91.413]

3. Can a pilot legally conduct flight operations with known inoperative equipment onboard?

Yes, under specific conditions. Part 91 describes acceptable methods for the operation of an aircraft with certain inoperative instruments and equipment that are not essential for safe flight; they are:

a. Operation of an aircraft with a minimum equipment list (MEL), as authorized by 14 CFR §91.213(a), or

b. Operation of an aircraft without a MEL under 14 CFR §91.213(d).

Exam Tip: Know this regulation well; unfamiliarity with 14 CFR §91.213 is a common weakness of applicants at all levels. You must demonstrate that you understand and know how to apply it.

[PA.IX.C, CA.IX.C; 14 CFR 91.213]

4. What limitations apply to aircraft operations conducted using the deferral provision of 14 CFR 91.213(d)?

When inoperative equipment is found during preflight or prior to departure, the decision should be to cancel the flight, to obtain maintenance prior to flight, or to defer the item or equipment. Maintenance deferrals are not used for equipment found inoperative while in flight. The manufacturer's pilot's operating handbook (POH)/airplane flight manual (AFM) procedures are to be used in those situations.

[PA.IX.C, CA.IX.C; FAA-H-8083-25]

5. During the preflight inspection in an aircraft that doesn't have a MEL, the pilot notices that an instrument or equipment item is inoperative. Describe how the pilot will determine if the aircraft is still airworthy for flight.

The pilot in this case will need to evaluate if the aircraft is able to be operated with the inoperative equipment. This will be done in the following order:

a. Is the inoperative equipment required for the day, night, or IFR flight requirements by regulation?

b. Is inoperative equipment allowed to be inoperative by any MEL or KOEL document that allows the pilot to operate in the specific conditions while inoperative?

c. Is the inoperative equipment required to be operational by an AD?

If the answer to any of items a, b, or c above is "yes," the aircraft is not considered airworthy and maintenance is required before it can be flown.

d. Is the equipment required according to the aircraft's type certificate data sheet?

e. Is the equipment such that it was installed in the equipment list as delivered from the manufacturer?

f. Is the equipment installed in accordance with a supplemental type certificate (STC)?

If the answer to any of items d, e, or f is "yes," a maintenance provider will need to address the concern and determine if the aircraft can be made airworthy. With this, a logbook entry would be required. If the equipment will not be fixed, the equipment will need to be disabled, placarded as "inoperative," and a logbook entry made.

g. Is the inoperative equipment able to be fixed by the pilot?

If the answer to item g is "yes," then the inoperative equipment is something that falls under the preventive maintenance allowances for a pilot to address, and the pilot may fix it and return the aircraft to an airworthy condition after properly logging the fix in the maintenance logs.

In a general sense, if some equipment is inoperative, and an MEL or KOEL does not give the pilot a path to operate with such equipment inoperative, it will require maintenance and documentation before the aircraft will be allowed to be operated.

[PA.I.B, CA.I.B; 14 CFR 91.213(d), FAA-H-8083-25]

6. What is a minimum equipment list (MEL)?

An MEL is a precise listing of instruments, equipment, and procedures that allows an aircraft to be operated under specific conditions with inoperative equipment. The MEL is the specific inoperative equipment document for a particular make and model aircraft by serial and registration numbers; e.g., BE-200, N12345. The FAA-approved MEL includes only those items of equipment that the FAA deems may be inoperative and still maintain an acceptable level of safety with appropriate conditions and limitations. A pilot should consider a MEL a "permission to operate with inoperative" list. Any items outside of this list and outside the conditions set forth should be considered required to be operational.

Note: Do not confuse an MEL with the aircraft's equipment list. They are not the same.

[PA.I.B, CA.I.B; FAA-H-8003-25]

7. For an aircraft with an approved MEL, explain the decision sequence a pilot would use after discovering the position lights are inoperative.

With an approved MEL, if the position lights were discovered inoperative prior to a daytime flight, the pilot would make an entry in the maintenance record or discrepancy record provided for that purpose. The item is then either repaired or deferred in accordance with the MEL. Upon confirming that daytime flight with inoperative position lights is acceptable in accordance with the provisions of the MEL, the pilot would leave the position lights switch OFF, open the circuit breaker (or whatever action is called for in the procedures document), and placard the position light switch as INOPERATIVE.

[PA.I.B, CA.I.B; FAA-H-8083-25]

8. Explain the limitations that apply to aircraft operations being conducted using an MEL.

The use of an MEL for a small, non-turbine-powered airplane operated under Part 91 allows for the deferral of inoperative items or equipment. The FAA considers an approved MEL to be a supplemental type certificate (STC) issued to an aircraft by serial number and registration number. Once an operator requests an MEL, and a Letter of Authorization (LOA) is issued by the FAA, then the MEL becomes mandatory for that aircraft. All maintenance deferrals must be done in accordance with the terms and conditions of the MEL and the operator-generated procedures document.

[PA.I.B, CA.I.B; FAA-H-8083-25]

9. Explain how you would "deactivate" an item or system that has become inoperative in your airplane. Can you deactivate any item or system in the airplane? What is required?

A pilot may only deactivate (placarding, disabling, and making a maintenance log entry) equipment that is allowed to be inoperative in accordance with an approved minimum equipment list (MEL) or kinds of operations equipment list (KOEL) or that is allowed under preventative maintenance allowances without assistance from a maintenance provider. Any other equipment that would be deactivated would require an FAA maintenance provider to determine if the aircraft was able to be operated in an airworthy condition and make appropriate notations in the maintenance logs after the equipment was disabled (or removed) and placarded appropriately.

[PA.I.B, CA.I.B; FAA-H-8083-25, 14 CFR Part 43 Appendix A]

B. Pilot Currency Requirements

1. When a pilot becomes multi-engine certificated, are they required to complete a flight review in a multi-engine aircraft to remain current for flight operations?

A pilot must complete a flight review in "an aircraft for which the pilot is rated." This does not say that a pilot must complete a flight review in *each* category and/or class of aircraft for which they are rated. A pilot who is single- and multi-engine rated could complete one flight review in the 24-month period in either of the aircraft classes and it would count for operating both classes of aircraft. A best practice for pilots might be to consider alternating their flight reviews to improve proficiency.

[PA.I.A, CA.I.A; 14 CFR 61.56]

2. What must a pilot do in regard to pilot currency to be able to take passengers in a multi-engine aircraft?

To take passengers, a pilot must complete three takeoffs and landings (at night if night flight will be conducted) within the preceding 90 days in "an aircraft of the same category, class, and type (if a type rating is required)." Because single- and multi-engine aircraft are in difference classes, a pilot who wants to fly a multi-engine aircraft would need to complete the takeoffs and landings in a multi-engine aircraft. In addition, while it may sound intuitive that a pilot could complete their takeoffs and landings in a more complex aircraft, doing so in a multi-engine aircraft would not count for takeoff and landing currency in a single-engine aircraft.

To apply this to some more examples, completing takeoffs and landings in a multi-engine aircraft that required a type rating, such as a Boeing 777, would count for currency for passenger carriage in a Beechcraft Baron, but not in the opposite direction. Likewise, takeoffs and landings in a Piper Seminole would not count for passenger carriage currency for a pilot who wanted to fly a Cessna 172.

[PA.I.A, CA.I.A; 14 CFR 61.57]

3. Must a pilot complete their instrument currency in a multi-engine aircraft to be able to fly in instrument conditions in a multi-engine aircraft?

Instrument currency is not limited to the required approaches or instrument proficiency check by category and/or class of aircraft. It is indicated that a pilot must complete their instrument proficiency in "an airplane, powered-lift, helicopter, or airship as appropriate." A pilot might also choose to use an appropriately certificated simulator to maintain instrument proficiency. Any combination of instrument activity that meets currency requirements in any of these aircraft or simulator will allow a pilot to establish instrument currency. As such, a pilot need not complete their instrument currency solely or even at all in a multi-engine aircraft to be able to fly under instrument flight rules in a multi-engine aircraft.

[PA.I.A, CA.I.A; 14 CFR 61.57]

4. A pilot can go beyond basic currency in a multi-engine aircraft through what efforts?

A pilot can go beyond basic training and currency requirements through continued practice of the tasks and skills in the ACS. A pilot may also choose to periodically have a qualified and proficient instructor work with them. This can be done more frequently than flight reviews every 24 calendar months. Some pilots will choose to select tasks from the FAA's WINGS program that relate to multi-engine flight proficiency and document their conduct and practice through the FAA Safety Program.

[PA.I.A, CA.I.A; FAA-P-8740-66]

5. What are some of the best ways a pilot can mitigate risks associated with multi-engine training?

a. Thoroughly brief simulated engine failures in advance. The pilot should know how such failures will be introduced and what action is expected in response. Unannounced engine failures are suitable only in testing and checking scenarios and when both pilots have agreed to such activity before the flight.

b. Low-altitude engine failure is never worth the risks involved. Multi-engine instructors should approach simulated engine failures below 400 feet AGL with extreme caution, and failures below 200 feet AGL should be reserved for simulators and training devices.

c. All simulated engine failures below 3,000 feet AGL should be accomplished by smoothly retarding the throttle.

d. Recognize that aircraft systems knowledge is critically important. Practice systems failures, too, including partial panel instrument training.

e. Do not alter the airplane configuration on the runway after landing unless there is a clear operational need to do so.

[PA.I.A, CA.I.A; FAA-P-8740-66]

C. Multi-Engine Operations Considerations

1. Is taxiing a multi-engine airplane significantly different than taxiing a single-engine airplane?

No, it is generally the same. The following general guidelines may be used:

a. Brakes and throttles are used to control momentum, using care not to ride the brakes by keeping engine power to a minimum.

b. Steering is done primarily with the steerable nose wheel.

c. Directional control may also be obtained through the use of differential power, if necessary.

d. Plan ahead. Multi-engine airplanes are heavier, larger, and more powerful. They require more time and distance to stop.

e. Also, due to aircraft size, the pilot's perspective may change, requiring additional vigilance to avoid obstacles, other aircraft, or bystanders.

[PA.II.D, CA.II.D; FAA-H-8083-3]

2. How can a pilot use differential power during taxiing?

While taxiing, a tight turn to the right, for example, may be accomplished by reducing power on the right engine and increasing power on the left engine while applying right rudder/brake. Also, in a crosswind condition, differential power assists in controlling direction. Power should be applied on the upwind engine, causing a turning moment away from the crosswind.

Note: Making sharp turns assisted by brakes and differential power can cause the airplane to pivot about a stationary inboard wheel and landing gear. The airplane was not designed for such abuse, and you should avoid doing this.

[PA.II.D, CA.II.D; FAA-H-8083-3]

3. How should checklists be used in multi-engine airplanes?

Checklist use is essential to the safe operation of a multi-engine airplane, and no flight should be conducted without one. Checklists need not be "do lists;" the proper actions can be accomplished and then the checklist used to quickly ensure all necessary tasks or actions have been completed. Certain immediate action items (such as the response to an engine failure in a critical phase of flight) should be committed to memory. After the action items are accomplished, and as workload permits, the pilot can then verify the action taken with a printed checklist.

[PA.II.B, CA.II.B; FAA-H-8083-3]

4. Why do some consider training and flying in a multi-engine aircraft to be associated with greater risk?

a. Multi-engine aircraft are heavier, faster, and the systems are typically more complex.

b. The increased performance and complexity of multi-engine aircraft require additional planning, judgment, and piloting skills.

c. At times, the workload for the pilot can be much higher than when flying a single-engine aircraft, increasing risk substantially, especially if the pilot has not maintained currency and proficiency.

d. When a malfunction or emergency occurs, the situation can deteriorate at a much faster rate than a comparable event or emergency in a single-engine airplane.

e. During flight training, substantially more time is devoted to emergency procedures with emphasis on one-engine-inoperative (OEI) procedures. Risk is increased.

[PA.X.A, CA.X.A; FAA-H-8083-2, FAA-H-8083-3]

5. Describe some of the factors that can result in failure to maintain situational awareness in a multi-engine aircraft.

a. Problems with handling a higher workload (task saturation).

b. Handling equipment malfunctions (fixation while troubleshooting).

c. Distractions and interruptions (other air traffic, ATC, navigation).

d. Insufficient aircraft knowledge and experience (confusion).

e. Dependency on advanced avionics (resulting in complacency and inattention).

[PA.X.A, CA.X.A; FAA-H-8083-2]

6. What are the three most critical phases of flight in a multi-engine airplane?

Takeoff, initial climb, and landing. During takeoff and climb, the aircraft is usually in its most vulnerable state—low altitude, slow airspeed, and heaviest operating weight. During landing, the aircraft is also operating at a relatively slow airspeed and low altitude, leaving little room for error.

[FAA-H-8083-3]

7. Provide an example of the takeoff briefing you will use today.

This is an example of a light twin takeoff control and performance briefing:

This will be a _____ (normal/short/soft field) takeoff from Runway _____ with a runway length of _____. The density altitude is _____ and the takeoff weight is _____. The required takeoff distance is _____ and the accelerate-stop distance is _____. The single-engine climb rate is _____ and the single-engine service ceiling is _____. V_{MC} is _____, V_R is _____, V_{XSE} is _____, V_{YSE} is _____, and V_Y is _____.

If an engine failure/abnormality occurs below _____ (V_{MC}) or _____ (V_R), I will retard the throttles and abort the takeoff.

If an engine failure/abnormality occurs after liftoff and the landing gear is down, I will close both throttles and land straight ahead.

If an engine failure/abnormality occurs after liftoff (at/above V_{XSE}) and the landing gear is retracted, I will follow the AFM procedures to:

- Control (pitch and power for V_{YSE}).
- Configure (flaps, gear, prop).
- Climb (maintain V_{YSE}; zero sideslip).
- Checklist (upon reaching 400 AGL).

[PA.II.F, CA.II.F; FAA Safety ALC-30]

8. What are the first and second priorities for a multi-engine pilot during the takeoff roll?

The multi-engine pilot's primary concern on all takeoffs is the attainment of the single-engine minimum control speed +5 knots prior to liftoff. Until this speed is achieved, directional control of the airplane in flight may be impossible after the failure of an engine, unless power is reduced immediately on the operating engine.

The multi-engine pilot's second concern on takeoff is the attainment of the best rate-of-climb speed (V_Y) in the least amount of time. This is the airspeed that will provide the greatest rate of climb with both engines operating. In the event of an engine failure, the single-engine best rate-of-climb speed (V_{YSE}) must be held. This will provide the best rate of climb when operating with one engine inoperative and propeller feathered (if possible), or the slowest rate of descent with the proper bank angle toward the operating engine.

[PA.II.F, CA.II.F; FAA Safety ALC-30]

9. Discuss a normal takeoff and climb procedure in a multi-engine airplane.

a. Use the manufacturer's recommended rotation speed (V_R) or lift-off speed (V_{LOF}), or, if no such speeds are published, use a minimum of 5 knots plus minimum control speed (V_{MC}) for V_R. As a rule, light twins should not be airborne before reaching V_{MC}.

b. Landing gear retraction should occur after a positive rate of climb is established but not before reaching a point from which a safe landing can no longer be made on the runway or overrun remaining.

c. After liftoff, gain altitude as rapidly as practicable. After leaving the ground, altitude gain is more important than achieving an enroute climb airspeed. Allow the airplane to accelerate in a shallow climb to attain V_Y, the best rate of climb speed when both engines are operating. If V_Y would result in a pitch attitude of more than 15 degrees, consider limiting the initial pitch attitude to 15 degrees to minimize control difficulty if an engine is lost.

d. Maintain V_Y until a safe single-engine maneuvering altitude, typically at least 400 feet AGL, has been achieved.

Note: On the takeoff roll, *never* attempt to become airborne before reaching V_{MC}. If an engine should fail below V_{MC}, the rudder will not be capable of counteracting the yaw resulting from asymmetric thrust, and the aircraft will not be controllable.

[PA.IV.A, CA.IV.A; FAA-P-8740-66]

10. Explain when you will retract the landing gear during takeoff. If you were taking off from an airport at 5,000 feet MSL with a 9,000-foot runway, when would you retract the gear?

Normally, the gear should be retracted when there is insufficient runway available for landing and after a positive rate of climb is established as indicated on the altimeter. If an excessive amount of runway is available, it would not be prudent to leave the landing gear down for an extended period of time and sacrifice climb performance and acceleration. In addition, in some multi-engine airplanes when operating in a high density-altitude environment, a positive rate of climb with the landing gear down is not possible. Waiting for a positive rate of climb under these conditions is not practicable.

[PA.IV.A, CA.IV.A; FAA-H-8083-3]

11. At what point in the descent and approach for landing should the before-landing checklist be completed?

The traffic pattern and approach are typically flown at somewhat higher indicated airspeeds in a multi-engine airplane than in most single-engine airplanes. The pilot should allow for this by getting an early start on the before-landing checklist, which provides time for proper planning, spacing, and thinking well ahead of the airplane.

[PA.IV.B, CA.IV.B; FAA-H-8083-3]

12. If a recommended airspeed is not provided by the manufacturer, what speed should be used for final approach to landing?

If a recommended speed is not furnished, the speed should be no slower than the single-engine best rate-of-climb speed (V_{YSE}) until short final with the landing assured, but in no case less than critical engine-out minimum control speed (V_{MC}).

[PA.IV.B, CA.IV.B; FAA-H-8083-3]

D. Performance and Limitations

1. Define the following speeds and their value for your aircraft: V_R, V_{LOF}, V_X, V_{XSE}, V_Y, V_{YSE}, V_{SSE}, V_{MC}, V_A, and V_{REF}.

V_R—Rotation speed. The speed at which back pressure is applied to rotate the airplane to a takeoff attitude.

V_{LOF}—Lift-off speed. The speed at which the airplane leaves the surface. (*Note:* Some manufacturers reference takeoff performance data to V_R, others to V_{LOF}.)

V_X—Best angle-of-climb speed. The speed at which the airplane will gain the greatest altitude for a given distance of forward travel.

V_{XSE}—Best angle-of-climb speed with one engine inoperative.

V_Y—Best rate-of-climb speed. The speed at which the airplane will gain the most altitude for a given unit of time.

V_{YSE}—Best rate-of-climb speed with one engine inoperative. Marked with a blue radial line on most airspeed indicators. Above the single-engine absolute ceiling, V_{YSE} yields the minimum rate of sink.

V_{SSE}—Safe, intentional one engine inoperative speed. Originally known as safe single-engine speed. It is the minimum speed to intentionally render the critical engine inoperative.

V_{MC}—Minimum control speed with the critical engine inoperative. Marked with a red radial line on most airspeed indicators. The minimum speed at which directional control can be maintained under a very specific set of circumstances outlined in 14 CFR Part 23, Airworthiness Standards.

V_A—Design maneuvering speed.

V_{REF}—Reference landing speed. An airspeed used for final approach that adjusts the normal approach speed for winds and gusty conditions. V_{REF} is 1.3 times the stall speed in the landing configuration.

[PA.I.F, CA.I.F; FAA-H-8083-3]

2. **When is the use of safe, intentional one engine inoperative speed (V_{SSE}) recommended?**

V_{SSE} is specified by the airplane manufacturer in the new handbooks and is the minimum speed at which to perform intentional simulation of failure of an engine. Use of V_{SSE} is intended to reduce the accident potential from loss of control after engine failure simulation at or near minimum control speed. Various engine failure demonstrations are necessary in training but should only be made at a safe altitude above the terrain and with the power reduction on one engine made at or above V_{SSE}.

[PA.I.F, CA.I.F; FAA-P-8740-66]

3. **Define *accelerate-stop distance*.**

The accelerate-stop distance is the runway length required to accelerate to a specified speed (either V_R or V_{LOF}, as specified by the manufacturer), experience an engine failure, and bring the airplane to a complete stop.

[PA.IX.E, CA.IX.E; FAA-H-8083-3]

4. **Is a takeoff advisable if the accelerate-stop distance exceeds the available runway distance? Why?**

While it is not prohibited for private carriage operations, it is not advisable for pilots to operate on runways shorter than a calculated accelerate-stop distance. In the event of an engine failure during the takeoff ground run, the pilot could not be certain that the aircraft could be brought to a full stop on the remaining runway. If a pilot has made a choice to operate from a runway shorter than the calculated accelerate-stop distance, the pilot should do so with understanding of the potential risk.

[PA.IX.E, CA.IX.E; FAA-H-8083-3]

5. Do the regulations require that the runway length be greater than the accelerate-stop distance?

Not all operations must comply with takeoff conditions under which a pilot is required to have calculated runway length be equal to or greater than the accelerate-stop distance. Most POHs/AFMs publish accelerate-stop distances only as an advisory. It becomes a limitation only when published in the limitations section of the POH/AFM or in commercial carriage operations that require adherence to these conditions as a part of operational requirements.

[PA.IX.E, CA.IX.E; FAA-H-8083-3]

6. What procedures are followed if the accelerate-stop distance exceeds the runway length and/or the density altitude is higher than the single-engine service ceiling?

If a takeoff is to be made, an alternate plan of action should be considered. It should include:

a. A review of emergency landing areas or other runways near the departure runway.

b. A review of engine-out performance speeds and procedures.

c. Due consideration to a reduction in baggage, fuel, and/or passengers to increase single-engine performance.

[PA.IX.E, CA.IX.E; FAA-H-8083-3]

7. Define *accelerate-go distance*.

Accelerate-go distance is the distance required to accelerate to either V_R or V_{LOF} (as specified by the manufacturer) and, assuming an engine failure at that instant, to continue the takeoff on the remaining engine and climb to a height of 50 feet.

[PA.IX.E, CA.IX.E; FAA-P-8740-66]

8. **During takeoff, what should you do if you experience a power loss on your left engine at lift-off speed? Your accelerate-go chart has indicated you have the required distance to continue the climb away from the runway and clear a 50-foot obstacle. Can you realistically identify, verify, feather, and clean up the airplane, and then establish a positive rate of climb away from the runway? What other factors could affect your decision to continue the takeoff?**

The multi-engine pilot must keep in mind that the accelerate-go distance, as long as it is, has only brought the airplane to a point a mere 50 feet above the takeoff elevation under ideal circumstances. To achieve even this meager climb, the pilot has to instantaneously recognize and react to an unanticipated engine failure, retract the landing gear, and identify and feather the correct engine, all the while maintaining precise airspeed control and bank angle as the airspeed is nursed to V_{YSE}. Assuming flawless airmanship thus far, the airplane has now arrived at a point little more than one wingspan above the terrain, assuming it was absolutely level and without obstructions. Density altitude and/or weight will also have a significant effect on climb performance.

[PA.IX.E, CA.IX.E; FAA-H-8083-3]

9. **Are accelerate-go distances available for all multi-engine aircraft?**

No. Not all manufacturers publish accelerate-go distances in their POH/AFM. When it is published, the figures will have been determined under ideal flight-testing conditions, and it is unlikely that this performance will be duplicated in service conditions.

Exam Tip: If the aircraft used for the practical exam has accelerate-stop/go data published in the POH/AFM, be thoroughly familiar with those charts and be capable of determining those distances for your aircraft on the day of your practical exam. Your examiner will also expect you to demonstrate how you will apply those distances during your pre-takeoff briefing. Also, remember to be skeptical of the performance data obtained from your aircraft's performance charts and add a significant margin for safety.

[PA.IX.E, CA.IX.E; FAA-H-8083-3]

10. In absence of the manufacturer's accelerate-stop distance information, how would you calculate your own accelerate-stop distance?

You can calculate your own accelerate-stop distances by running the aircraft up to takeoff speed and then bringing it to a stop. (Make sure you start these tests on a good, long runway.) Do this several times at maximum gross weight while counting runway lights (the airport operator can tell you the distance between lights) and you'll get a good ballpark figure for an accelerate-stop distance. Then use that figure in your future takeoff planning.

Note: You can also calculate a rough estimate of your accelerate-stop distance by adding the normal takeoff distance to the landing distance over a 50-foot obstacle. Factor in a significant margin for real-world performance (such as 50 percent) to the result and you will have a rough estimate of your accelerate-stop distance.

[PA.IX.E, CA.IX.E; FAA-P-8740-66]

11. Explain the risks associated with performing takeoffs on a short runway in a multi-engine airplane.

The risks associated with taking off from a short runway in a multi-engine aircraft include all of the same risks that might be associated with a single-engine aircraft, but with some additional factors. Decision-making in a multi-engine aircraft will additionally include factors related to failure of a single engine during the takeoff roll or after liftoff. During a takeoff roll before liftoff, this will result in yawing of the aircraft and potential controllability concerns while still on the ground as well as reduced performance to continue a takeoff that may make clearing obstacles and climbing no longer possible. In the case of a single engine failure after liftoff, the significant reduction in power may not allow a pilot to climb at a sufficient rate to meet gradient requirements, or in some cases, even maintain altitude, especially if configuration changes are not made quickly. Added to this is the risk of a V_{MC} condition while the pilot is at a V_X or V_Y speed that may be at or near V_{MC} speed. A pilot is best served to transition to V_{YSE} or a greater climb speed as altitude and obstacle clearance allows during any takeoff from short fields in a multi-engine aircraft to mitigate as many risks as possible.

[PA.IX.F, CA.IX.F, PA.IX.E, CA.IX.E; FAA-H-8083-3]

12. What performance factors should be considered when planning a takeoff in a multi-engine airplane?

Know the POH/AFM performance capabilities for your airplane under the proposed flight conditions and factor in significant margins to adjust for real-world performance. Review the following:

a. Weight and balance.

b. Normal takeoff ground run distance.

c. Ground run distance required to clear a 50-foot obstacle.

d. Accelerate-stop and accelerate-go distances.

e. Existing density altitude and single-engine service ceiling.

f. Expected one engine inoperative rate of climb.

[PA.IV.A, CA.IV.A; FAA-H-8083-3, FAA-P-8740-66]

13. Describe several preflight actions you can take to mitigate risk during a takeoff and departure in a multi-engine airplane.

Competent pilots plan the takeoff in sufficient detail to be able to take immediate action if an engine fails during the takeoff process. The pilot should:

a. Evaluate runway conditions including length, slope, and contamination.

b. Evaluate terrain and obstructions for obstacle clearance. Trees, powerlines, towers, rising terrain, etc., may become obstructions during an emergency. Use VFR charts (sectional, TACs) and instrument charts (SIAPs, DPs) to identify these.

c. Consider the time of departure and meteorological conditions; fewer options are available when departing at night or with low ceilings.

d. Consider aircraft performance (all-engine and OEI) to ensure terrain and obstacle avoidance.

e. Conduct a takeoff briefing—review emergency procedures, V-speeds, plan of action.

f. Have an alternate plan of action in the event of an emergency.

[PA.IV.A, CA.IV.A; FAA-H-8083-2, FAA-H-8083-3]

14. Explain how an increase in density altitude will affect the performance of a multi-engine airplane.

An increase in density altitude will result in:

a. Increased takeoff distance (greater takeoff TAS required).

b. Increased accelerate-stop and accelerate-go distance (engine produces less power, prop less efficient, produces less thrust).

c. Increased true airspeed on approach and landing (same IAS).

d. Increased landing roll distance due to higher true airspeed.

e. Decreased all-engine and one engine inoperative rate of climb.

f. Decreased all-engine and single-engine service ceilings.

g. Decreased V_{MC} (and at some altitudes, V_{MC} and V_S will be the same).

[PA.I.F, CA.I.F; FAA-H-8083-3, FAA-P-8740-2]

15. What are several options that should be considered if attempting a short-field takeoff in a light-twin aircraft that has a best angle-of-climb speed that is less than 5 knots higher than V_{MC}?

Engine failure on takeoff, particularly with obstructions, is compounded by the low airspeeds and steep climb attitudes used in short-field takeoffs. V_X and V_{XSE} are often perilously close to V_{MC}, leaving scant margin for error in the event of engine failure as V_{XSE} is assumed. If flaps are used for takeoff, the engine failure situation becomes even more critical due to the additional drag incurred. If V_X is less than 5 knots higher than V_{MC}, give strong consideration to reducing useful load or using another runway in order to increase the takeoff margins so that a short-field technique will not be required.

[PA.IV.E, CA.IV.E; FAA-H-8083-3]

16. **What four main factors determine climb performance?**

    Airspeed—Too little or too much will decrease climb performance.

    Drag—Created by gear, flaps, cowl flaps, propeller, and airspeed.

    Power—The amount available in excess of that needed for level flight.

    Weight—Passengers, baggage, and fuel load greatly affect climb performance.

    [PA.II.F, CA.II.F; FAA-P-8740-66]

17. **Excluding an engine failure, what other abnormalities would cause you to abort a takeoff either before rotation or after rotation/liftoff?**

    During a takeoff roll, a pilot may encounter a number of abnormalities other than an engine failure that might cause them to abort the takeoff. Runway incursions, less-than-expected performance, contaminated runway conditions, changing wind conditions, blown tires, instructions from ATC to abort, or recognition of any other abnormality are only a few that might occur. A pilot might even choose to abort for a developing passenger condition. In any instance, a pilot should abort a takeoff when it is not clear that the takeoff can be continued safely. In some instances, this is even advisable when it will cause the pilot to run off the end of the runway if sufficient runway is not still remaining. Low-energy accidents result in more survivable accidents than high-energy accidents.

    [PA.IV.A, CA.IX.A; FAA-H-8083-3]

18. **Overall climb performance is reduced by what value in an engine-out emergency? Why?**

    Climb performance depends on an excess of power over that required for level flight. Loss of power from one engine obviously represents a 50-percent loss of power, but in virtually all light twins, climb performance is reduced by at least 80 percent. The amount of power required for level flight depends on how much drag must be overcome to sustain level flight. It is obvious that if drag is increased because the gear and flaps are down and the propeller is windmilling, more power will be required. What may not be so obvious, however, is the fact that drag increases as the square of the airspeed while the power required to maintain that speed increases as the cube of the airspeed.

[PA.IX.F, CA.IX.F; FAA-P-8740-66]

19. What operational advantages are achieved through use of a cruise-climb airspeed versus a best rate-of-climb airspeed during an extended climb?

a. A higher ground speed (forward speed) will be achieved, reducing the total time en route (usually an important factor in cross-country trips).

b. Only a small reduction in the rate of climb will occur.

c. An increase in forward visibility is achieved during climb-out.

d. Engine cooling is increased due to a higher forward speed.

[PA.II.F, CA.II.F; FAA-P-8740-66]

20. Why are some multi-engine aircraft required to have performance capabilities that require a positive single-engine climb rate?

In the interest of safety, the FAA requires that all turboprop aircraft, turbojet aircraft, large aircraft (10 or more passengers), or aircraft involved in air taxi operations be required to demonstrate continued takeoff capability with one engine inoperative.

[PA.IX.F, CA.IX.F; 14 CFR Part 23]

21. What are the single-engine climb performance requirements for reciprocating engine-powered multi-engine airplanes?

The 14 CFR Part 23 requirements are as follows:

a. *For aircraft that have a maximum takeoff weight that exceeds 6,000 pounds and/or a V_{S0} that is greater than 61 knots*—The single-engine rate of climb in feet per minute at 5,000 feet MSL must be equal to at least $0.027 V_{S0}^2$. For airplanes type-certificated February 4, 1991, or after, the climb requirement is expressed in terms of a climb gradient, 1.5 percent. The climb gradient is not a direct equivalent of the $0.027 V_{S0}^2$ formula. The date of type certification should not be confused with the airplane's model year; the type certification basis of many multi-engine airplanes dates back to the Civil Aviation Regulations (CAR) 3.

b. *For an aircraft that has a maximum takeoff weight that is less than 6,000 pounds and a V_{S0} of less than 61 knots*—The single-engine rate of climb at 5,000 feet MSL must simply be determined. The rate of climb could be a negative number. There is no requirement for a single-engine positive rate of climb at 5,000 feet or any other altitude. For light-twins type-certificated February 4, 1991, or after, the single-engine climb gradient (positive or negative) is simply determined.

[PA.IX.F, CA.IX.F; FAA-H-8083-3]

22. Define the term *service ceiling*.

The service ceiling is the maximum density altitude where the best rate-of-climb airspeed will produce a 100 feet-per-minute climb at maximum weight while in a clean configuration with maximum continuous power.

[PA.I.F, CA.I.F; FAA-H-8083-25]

23. What factors affect the effective service ceiling of a multi-engine airplane?

The service ceiling will be affected by:

a. Weight
b. Pressure altitude
c. Temperature

Note: The newer POHs/AFMs show service ceiling as a function of weight, pressure altitude, and temperature, while the older ones frequently use density altitude for this.

[PA.I.F, CA.I.F; FAA-P-8740-66]

24. Define the term *absolute ceiling*.

The absolute ceiling is the altitude at which a climb is no longer possible. It is also the density altitude where V_X and V_Y are equal.

[PA.I.F, CA.I.F; FAA-H-8083-3]

25. Define *single-engine service ceiling.*

The single-engine service ceiling is the altitude at which a twin-engine airplane can no longer climb at a rate greater than 50 feet per minute with one engine inoperative.

[PA.I.F, CA.I.F; FAA-H-8083-3]

26. Define the term *climb gradient.*

Climb gradient can be expressed as a percentage or as a ratio. It is most frequently expressed in terms of altitude gain per 100 feet of horizontal distance, where it is stated as a percentage. A 1.5 percent climb gradient is an altitude gain of one and one-half feet per 100 feet of horizontal travel. Climb gradient may also be expressed as a function of altitude gain per nautical mile, or as a ratio of the horizontal distance to the vertical distance (50:1, for example).

[PA.I.F, CA.I.F; FAA-H-8083-3]

27. Is a takeoff advisable if the density altitude at an airport is higher than the single-engine service ceiling?

No. Available alternatives are few since the aircraft would be unable to climb or even maintain altitude in the event of an engine failure on takeoff. Know before you take the runway whether you can maintain control and climb out if you lose an engine while the gear is still down.

[PA.I.F, CA.I.F; FAA-H-8083-3]

28. Do the regulations prohibit a pilot from attempting a takeoff in a multi-engine airplane if the airport density altitude is higher than the single-engine service ceiling?

No, if operations are being conducted under Part 91, there is no regulation prohibiting the pilot from doing so. However, in the event of an engine failure, it is unlikely the aircraft would be able to climb or potentially even leave the ground.

[PA.I.F, CA.I.F; 14 CFR Part 91]

29. **When you are planning a departure from an airport with a high density altitude, what aircraft performance value should you always compare with the existing density altitude?**

When planning a departure from an airport with a high density altitude, you should always compare the existing density altitude with the aircraft's published takeoff performance charts or tables. Specifically, you should compare the density altitude with the aircraft's takeoff distance performance values.

Density altitude is a measure of air density in the atmosphere, taking into account both altitude and temperature. High density altitude conditions, typically found at high elevations or in hot weather, reduce aircraft performance by decreasing air density, which in turn affects engine power and aerodynamic lift.

By comparing the density altitude with the aircraft's takeoff performance values from the performance charts, pilots can determine if the available runway length and aircraft performance are sufficient for a safe takeoff. If the density altitude exceeds the aircraft's performance limitations, the pilot may need to adjust the takeoff procedure, such as reducing aircraft weight, using a longer runway, or delaying departure until conditions improve. This comparison ensures that the aircraft can safely achieve the required takeoff performance under the existing atmospheric conditions.

[PA.I.F, CA.I.F; FAA-H-8083-3]

30. **If an engine failure occurs on takeoff at a field where the density altitude is higher than the single-engine service ceiling, what performance can be expected with one engine out?**

None. The aircraft would be unable to climb or potentially even leave the ground because the aircraft engine would be unable to produce a positive performance value.

[PA.I.F, CA.I.F; FAA-H-8083-3]

31. During flight planning, what important consideration should be made concerning the single-engine service ceiling as related to the enroute portion of a flight?

The single-engine service ceiling chart should always be used during flight planning to determine whether the airplane, as loaded, can maintain the minimum enroute altitude (MEA) if IFR, or terrain clearance if VFR, following an engine failure.

[PA.X.C, CA.X.C; FAA-P-8740-66]

32. What is meant by the term *drift down*?

If an airplane is above its single-engine absolute ceiling at the time of engine failure, it will slowly lose altitude. The airplane will then "drift down" to its single-engine absolute ceiling. The pilot should maintain V_{YSE} to minimize the rate of altitude loss. The drift-down rate will be greatest immediately following the failure and will decrease as the single-engine ceiling is approached. Takeoffs at airports that are higher than the drift-down altitude should be considered carefully with regard to how an engine failure during climb-out would be managed.

[PA.X.C, CA.X.C; FAA-H-8083-3]

33. Be capable of determining the following information for your aircraft.

a. Total takeoff distance required to clear a 50-foot obstacle.

b. Accelerate-stop distance when an engine failure occurs at takeoff decision speed.

c. Accelerate-go distance (if available) when an engine failure occurs at V_R or V_{LOF}.

d. All-engine and single-engine climb performance.

e. Single-engine service ceiling.

f. Single-engine inoperative enroute performance at planned cruising altitude.

g. Fuel consumption, range, and endurance.

h. Time and point-of-descent from cruising altitude to pattern altitude.

i. Normal landing distance and total distance to land over a 50-foot obstacle.

Note: Be skeptical when referencing your aircraft's performance charts and make sure you read the fine print. Always consider the necessity to compensate for the performance numbers if the aircraft and/or engines are older or piloting skills are below average. For one engine inoperative operations, turbulence, wind gusts, engine and propeller wear, or poor technique in airspeed, bank angle, and rudder control can all easily negate even a 200 feet per minute rate of climb.

[PA.I.F, CA.I.F; AFM]

E. Weight and Balance

1. What performance characteristics will be adversely affected when an aircraft has been overloaded? In what way will each be affected?

a. Higher takeoff speed.

b. Longer takeoff run.

c. Reduced rate and angle of climb.

d. Lower maximum altitude.

e. Shorter range.

f. Reduced cruising speed.

g. Reduced maneuverability.

h. Higher stalling speed.

i. Higher approach and landing speed.

j. Longer landing roll.

k. Excessive weight on the nose wheel.

[PA.I.F, CA.I.F; FAA-H-8083-25]

2. What effect does a forward center of gravity have on an aircraft's flight characteristics?

Higher stall speed—The stalling angle of attack is reached at a higher speed due to increased wing loading.

Slower cruise speed—Increased drag; greater angle of attack required to maintain altitude.

More stable—When angle of attack is increased, airplane tends to reduce angle of attack; longitudinal stability.

Lower V_{MC}—Rudder is more effective.

(continued)

Greater back elevator pressure required—Longer takeoff roll; higher approach speeds and problems with landing flare resulting in longer landing distances.

[PA.I.F, CA.I.F; FAA-H-8083-3]

3. **What effect does an aft center of gravity have on an aircraft's flight characteristics?**

Lower stall speed—Less wing loading.

Higher cruise speed—Reduced drag; smaller angle of attack required to maintain altitude.

Less stable—Stall and spin recovery are more difficult; when angle of attack is increased, it tends to result in additional increased angle of attack.

Higher V_{MC}—Rudder is less effective.

[PA.I.F, CA.I.F; FAA-H-8083-3]

4. **What are the definitions of the terms *standard empty weight*, *basic empty weight*, and *licensed empty weight*?**

Standard empty weight (GAMA)—The weight of a standard airplane including unusable fuel, full operating fluids, and full oil.

Basic empty weight (GAMA)—The standard empty weight plus optional equipment. Optional equipment includes the weight of all equipment installed beyond standard.

Licensed empty weight—This includes the standard airplane, optional equipment, full hydraulic fluid, unusable fuel, and undrainable oil.

Note: The major difference between the two formats (GAMA and the older method) is that basic empty weight includes full oil, and licensed empty weight does not.

[PA.I.F, CA.I.F; FAA-H-8083-3]

5. **Define the following terms: *maximum ramp weight*, *maximum takeoff weight*, *maximum landing weight*, and *zero fuel weight*.**

Maximum ramp weight—Some multi-engine airplanes have a ramp weight, which is in excess of the maximum takeoff weight. The ramp weight is an allowance for fuel burned during taxi and runup, permitting a takeoff at full maximum takeoff weight.

Maximum takeoff weight—The maximum allowable weight at the start of the takeoff run.

Maximum landing weight—The greatest weight that an aircraft normally is allowed to have when it lands. This requires preflight planning of fuel burn to ensure that the airplane weight upon arrival at its destination will be at or below the maximum landing weight. In the event of an emergency requiring an immediate landing, the pilot should recognize that the structural margins designed into the airplane are not fully available when over the landing weight.

Zero fuel weight—The maximum allowable weight of the airplane and payload, assuming there is no usable fuel on board. The actual airplane is not devoid of fuel at the time of loading, but this is merely a calculation that assumes it was. If a zero fuel weight limitation is published, then all weight in excess of that figure must consist of usable fuel. The purpose of a zero fuel weight is to limit load forces on the cabin floor of the aircraft, the wing spars, or other surfaces with heavy fuselage loads.

[PA.I.F, CA.I.F; FAA-H-8083-3]

6. Define the term *payload*.

Payload is the weight of occupants, cargo, and baggage. Assuming maximum fuel, the payload is the difference between the weight of the fueled airplane and the maximum takeoff weight.

[PA.I.F, CA.I.F; FAA-H-8083-3]

7. Be capable of calculating a weight and balance computation for your aircraft using the following data. Also, calculate a weight and balance computation after 2 hours of flight.

a. Pilot and copilot (be sure to obtain the examiner's weight)
b. Passengers
c. Fuel and oil
d. Baggage

[PA.I.F, CA.I.F; AFM]

8. What happens to the center of gravity (CG) of the airplane as fuel is burned in flight?

The effect of fuel burn during flight depends on the positioning of fuel tanks in relation to forward or aft, or lateral position. Fuel tanks that are forward of the CG would cause the CG to shift aftward if they were burned first, and conversely fuel tanks that are aft of the CG would cause a forward shift in CG if they were burned first. In most general aviation aircraft, including multi-engine aircraft, fuel is centrally located at the CG position so that the CG position remains centrally located during a long flight while fuel is burned and the overall weight of the aircraft changes.

Be aware of the positioning of fuel tanks in your aircraft and determine if fuel burn over time does affect the CG position. CG position may also shift laterally and cause a roll motion if one side is reduced more than the other. This is most commonly experienced in a multi-engine aircraft if an engine shutdown is experienced and the pilot does not cross-feed fuel over time.

[PA.I.F, CA.I.F; POH]

9. Is it possible to conduct a safe flight in your aircraft when it is loaded with the maximum passengers, bags, and fuel on board?

Most aircraft have weight limitations that may limit a pilot from filling all the seats, baggage areas, and fuel tanks. A careful calculation will be needed to determine based on desired passenger capacity if the aircraft can be filled and remain within gross weight, takeoff weight, and zero fuel weight limitations while also adding sufficient fuel for a desired flight. In many cases, as passenger or baggage demands increase, the pilot will need to sacrifice fuel loads and be required to make shorter flight legs, stopping for fuel. The other option would be to add more fuel and decrease cabin passenger loading and/or baggage carriage.

Refer carefully to weight and balance charts and practice with multiple loading scenarios to become familiar with what combinations might be possible. Be sure to check if the loading also stays within forward or aft limitations in the loading configurations.

[PA.I.F, CA.I.F; POH]

Aircraft
Systems

2

The following questions and answers deal with the systems that are generally found on multi-engine airplanes. For accuracy, you should review your aircraft's POH/AFM.

A. Primary Flight Controls

1. What are the primary flight controls on a multi-engine airplane?

The primary control systems consist of those that are required to safely control an airplane during flight. These include the ailerons, elevator (or stabilator), and rudder.

[PA.I.G, CA.I.G; FAA-H-8083-25]

2. Briefly describe the function of the following flight controls: ailerons, elevator, and rudder.

Ailerons — Control roll about the longitudinal axis. Ailerons are connected by cables, bellcranks, pulleys, or push-pull tubes to each other and to the control wheel.

Elevator — Controls pitch about the lateral axis. The elevator is connected to the control column in the flight deck by a series of mechanical linkages.

Rudder — Controls movement of the airplane about its vertical axis. It is a movable surface hinged to a fixed surface attached to the vertical stabilizer, or fin.

[PA.I.G, CA.I.G; FAA-H-8083-25]

3. What is a stabilator?

A stabilator is a one-piece horizontal stabilizer that pivots from a central hinge point that is extremely sensitive to control inputs and aerodynamic loads; therefore, anti-servo tabs are incorporated on the trailing edge to decrease sensitivity. In addition, a balance weight is usually incorporated ahead of the main spar. The balance weight may project into the empennage or may be incorporated on the forward portion of the stabilator tips.

[PA.I.G, CA.I.G; FAA-H-8083-25]

4. Explain the procedures a pilot would use in responding to a jammed elevator.

If an elevator becomes jammed, resulting in a total loss of elevator control movement, various combinations of power and flap extension offer a limited amount of pitch control. Trim mechanisms can also be useful in the event of an inflight primary control failure. A successful landing under these conditions, however, is problematic.

[PA.I.G, CA.I.G; FAA-H-8083-3]

B. Secondary Flight Controls

1. What are the different secondary flight controls on an aircraft?

Wing flaps, leading edge devices, spoilers, and trim systems constitute the secondary control system and improve the performance characteristics of the airplane or relieve the pilot of excessive control forces.

[PA.I.G, CA.I.G; FAA-H-8083-25]

2. What is the purpose of flaps and what are the four most common types found on aircraft?

Flaps attached to the trailing edge of the wing increase both lift and induced drag for any given angle of attack. Flaps allow a compromise between high cruising speed and low landing speed, because they may be extended when needed and retracted into the wing's structure when not needed. The four most common types are plain, split, slotted, and Fowler flaps.

[PA.I.G, CA.I.G; FAA-H-8083-25]

3. Describe the various types of flap systems installed on aircraft.

Plain flap—The simplest of the four types. When extended, it increases the airfoil camber, which results in a significant increase in the coefficient of lift as well as drag at a given angle of attack and moves the center of pressure aft on the airfoil, resulting in a nose-down pitching moment.

Split flap—Deflected from the lower surface of the airfoil, it produces a slightly greater increase in lift than does the plain flap.

However, more drag is created because of the turbulent air pattern produced behind the airfoil.

Slotted flap—The most popular flap on airplanes today, it increases the lift coefficient significantly more than plain or split flaps. The slotted flap hinge is located below the lower surface of the flap, and when the flap is lowered, it forms a duct between the flap well in the wing and the leading edge of the flap. With the flap lowered, high-energy air from the lower surface is ducted to the flap's upper surface. The high-energy air from the slot accelerates the upper surface boundary layer and delays airflow separation, providing a higher coefficient of lift.

Fowler flap—A type of slotted flap that not only changes the camber of the wing but also increases the wing area. The flap slides backward on tracks in the first portion of extension, significantly increasing lift with little additional drag. As extension continues, the flap deflects downward, increasing drag with little additional increase in lift.

[PA.I.G, CA.I.G; FAA-H-8083-25]

4. How are flaps extended and retracted?

The flap system may be an electric, hydraulic, or manual system. The most common type of system uses a wing flap switch lever and electric motor to actuate and drive the flaps to the extended or retracted position. A single electric motor utilizing push/pull rods, two interconnected bellcranks, and cables drives both flaps to the selected position. The wing flap system circuit is usually protected by either a push-to-reset circuit breaker or a fuse.

[PA.I.G, CA.I.G; POH/AFM]

5. What is an asymmetric/split flap condition?

This condition occurs when one flap deploys or retracts while the other remains in position, resulting in a pronounced roll toward the wing with the least flap deflection. The yaw caused by the additional drag created by the extended flap requires substantial opposite rudder, resulting in a cross-control condition. Almost full aileron may be required to maintain a wings-level attitude, especially at the reduced airspeed necessary for approach and landing.

[PA.I.G, CA.I.G; FAA-H-8083-3, POH/AFM]

6. What are several types of aircraft trim systems?

Trim tabs—Adjustable surfaces attached to the trailing edge of the elevator or rudder. They are manually or electrically operated by a small, vertically or horizontally mounted control wheel. Placing the trim control in the full nose-down position moves the tab to its full up position.

Balance tabs—These look like trim tabs and are hinged in approximately the same places. The essential difference between the two is that the balancing tab is coupled to the control surface rod so that when the primary control surface is moved in any direction, the tab automatically moves in the opposite direction.

Anti-servo tabs—These tabs decrease the sensitivity of the stabilator and also function as a trim device to relieve control pressure and maintain the stabilator in the desired position. The fixed end of the linkage is on the opposite side of the surface from the horn on the tab, and when the trailing edge of the stabilator moves up, the linkage forces the trailing edge of the tab up.

Ground adjustable tabs—A non-movable metal trim tab on the rudder that can be bent in one direction or the other while on the ground to apply a trim force to the rudder. The correct displacement is determined by a trial-and-error process.

[PA.I.G, CA.I.G; FAA-H-8083-25]

7. Explain the procedures you would use in the event you experience a trim system or autopilot failure (or runaway trim).

a. *Autopilot disconnect switch*—The first and closest method of disconnecting a malfunctioning autopilot; typically mounted on the control yoke.

b. *Mode buttons*—Found on the autopilot control panel. Using these may be effective; however, there are some failures (shorted relays, wires, etc.) that remove control of the servo actuator from the control unit itself.

c. *Circuit breakers*—Find and pull the circuit breakers that interrupt power to both the trim and autopilot systems. Some trim systems have separate circuit breakers for trim motors that operate different control surfaces (roll, pitch, and yaw).

(continued)

d. *Control yoke*—Most autopilot and trim systems use a simple clutch mechanism that allows you to overpower the system by forcing the control yoke in the desired direction. This is usually checked during the after-start, pre-takeoff, run-up checks.

Note: Ensure that you understand all functions and equipment that will be affected when pulling any circuit breaker. A circuit breaker installed in an aircraft can supply power to more functions than the label implies.

[PA.I.G, CA.I.G; FAA-H-8083-16]

8. Describe how the stall warning system works.

The stall warning system in an aircraft is designed to alert pilots when the aircraft is approaching an aerodynamic stall—a condition where the wings lose lift due to exceeding the critical angle of attack. The stall warning system typically operates based on the principle of detecting changes in airflow over the wings.

Angle of attack sensors—The stall warning system employs angle of attack (AOA) sensors or vanes mounted on the aircraft's wings. These sensors measure the angle between the wing's chord line and the relative airflow, indicating how close the wing is to its critical angle of attack.

Stall warning device—When the AOA sensors detect that the wing's angle of attack is approaching the critical threshold, a stall warning device is activated. This device may consist of an audible horn, a visual indicator, or both, located within the flight deck where the pilot can easily see or hear it.

Activation threshold—The stall warning system is designed to activate before the aircraft actually stalls, providing the pilot with a timely warning to take corrective action. The activation threshold is typically set slightly above the angle of attack that corresponds to the stall angle, allowing for a margin of safety.

[PA.I.G, CA.I.G; POH/AFM]

C. Powerplant and Propeller

1. Define the term *reciprocating engine*.

The name is derived from the back-and-forth, or reciprocating, movement of the pistons. It is this motion that produces the mechanical energy needed to accomplish work.

[PA.I.G, CA.I.G; FAA-H-8083-25]

2. What are the two types of induction systems used in small aircraft?

a. *Carburetor systems* mix the fuel and air in the carburetor before the mixture enters the intake manifold.

b. *Fuel-injection systems* mix the fuel and air immediately before entry into each cylinder or inject fuel directly into each cylinder.

Note: Be able to describe what the symptoms would be of carburetor icing in a carbureted aircraft. Know that if the aircraft is equipped with a constant-speed propeller, a drop in RPM will not be the first indication; it will be a drop in manifold pressure. Understand under what atmospheric conditions carburetor icing is most likely to occur.

[PA.I.G, CA.I.G; FAA-H-8083-25]

3. When describing an engine, what does the term *horizontally opposed* refer to?

A horizontally opposed engine always has an even number of cylinders, since a cylinder on one side of the crankcase "opposes" a cylinder on the other side. The majority of these engines are air cooled and usually are mounted in a horizontal position when installed on fixed-wing airplanes.

[PA.I.G, CA.I.G; FAA-H-8083-25]

4. When describing an aircraft engine, what do the terms *direct-drive* and *normally aspirated* mean?

Direct-drive means that the propeller is bolted to, and turns at the same speed as, the crankshaft. No reduction gearing is used.

Normally aspirated means that the engine has no supercharger or turbocharger to maintain sea level atmospheric pressure at higher altitudes, and therefore its maximum available power decreases with altitude.

[PA.I.G, CA.I.G; FAA-P-8740-13]

5. Briefly describe how engine ignition is provided.

Engine ignition is provided by two engine-driven magnetos and two spark plugs per cylinder. The ignition system is completely independent of the aircraft electrical system. The magnetos are engine-driven, self-contained units supplying electrical current without using an external source of current.

[PA.II.C, CA.II.C; POH/AFM]

6. Define the term *brake horsepower*.

The power delivered at the propeller shaft (main drive or main output) of an aircraft engine.

[PA.I.G, CA.I.G; FAA-H-8083-25]

7. When conducting a magneto drop-off check on the ground, why will you see a drop in RPM on an airplane equipped with a constant-speed propeller?

During a magneto drop-off check on the ground, where one magneto is momentarily disabled to assess engine performance, aircraft equipped with a constant-speed propeller will typically experience a drop in RPM. This drop occurs due to the loss of ignition spark from the disabled magneto, resulting in incomplete combustion within the engine cylinders.

When the magneto is disabled, the spark plugs connected to that magneto stop firing, causing the affected cylinders to receive no ignition source. As a result, the air-fuel mixture in those cylinders is not ignited properly, leading to a reduction in engine power output and, consequently, a decrease in RPM.

In a constant-speed propeller system, the governor adjusts the propeller pitch to maintain a constant engine RPM set by the pilot. However, when one magneto is disabled, the engine experiences a decrease in power, causing the governor to adjust the propeller pitch angle to try to maintain the set RPM. The combination of reduced power output and propeller pitch adjustment leads to a noticeable drop in RPM during the magneto drop-off check.

[PA.I.G, CA.I.G; POH/AFM]

8. When performing a magneto check or exercising the propeller prior to departure (constant-speed propeller), you notice that as the RPM drops, the manifold pressure rises slightly. Why does the manifold pressure rise?

When performing a magneto check or exercising the propeller in an aircraft with a constant-speed propeller prior to departure, it's not uncommon to observe a slight rise in manifold pressure as the RPM drops. This phenomenon occurs due to the interaction between the propeller pitch angle and engine power output.

As the RPM decreases during the magneto check or propeller exercise, the constant-speed propeller blades tend to increase their pitch angle. This increase in pitch results in a greater load on the engine, which requires an increase in manifold pressure to maintain the same power output. The engine compensates for the increased load by adjusting the throttle to increase manifold pressure.

Additionally, the decrease in RPM reduces the airflow through the engine, leading to a slight increase in air density within the intake manifold. This increase in air density also contributes to the rise in manifold pressure.

Overall, the rise in manifold pressure during a magneto check or propeller exercise is a normal response of the engine and propeller system to changes in RPM and pitch angle.

[PA.I.G, CA.I.G; FAA-H-8083-25]

9. **Define the term *manifold pressure*.**

   Manifold pressure is the absolute pressure of the air-fuel mixture within the intake manifold, usually indicated in inches of mercury.

   [PA.I.G, CA.I.G; FAA-H-8083-3]

10. **Why does a non-turbocharged airplane experience a loss in manifold pressure (power) as it gains altitude?**

    The loss occurs because the same volume of air going into the engine's induction system gradually decreases in density as altitude increases. When the volume of air in the manifold decreases, it causes a loss of power. This will occur at the rate of approximately 1 inch of manifold pressure for each 1,000-foot gain in altitude.

    [PA.I.G, CA.I.G; FAA-H-8083-3]

11. **Describe what the manifold pressure gauge will indicate in the following situations:**
    - **On the ground, engine not running.**
    - **On the ground, engine running.**
    - **In the air, engine failure, loss of power.**

    On the ground, engine not running—The manifold pressure gauge will indicate ambient air pressure (i.e., 29.92 inHg).

    On the ground, engine running—The manifold pressure gauge will decrease to a value less than ambient pressure (i.e., idle at 12 inHg).

    In the air, engine failure, loss of power—The manifold pressure gauge will indicate an increase in manifold pressure to a value corresponding to the ambient air pressure at the altitude where the failure occurred.

    [PA.I.G, CA.I.G; FAA-H-8083-25]

12. **When starting an engine, will the manifold pressure gauge indicate an increase or decrease in manifold pressure? Why?**

    When starting an aircraft engine, the manifold pressure gauge may indicate an increase or decrease in manifold pressure depending on several factors related to engine operation and airflow dynamics.

As the engine starts, the suction generated by the turning propeller draws air into the intake manifold. Initially, the throttle is closed, restricting the airflow into the engine. However, the suction from the propeller creates a lower pressure zone within the intake manifold, causing the manifold pressure gauge to indicate a temporary increase in pressure as air rushes into the manifold.

Once the engine starts and the throttle is opened slightly, the airflow into the engine increases, causing the pressure within the intake manifold to stabilize or even decrease from the initial peak. This decrease occurs because the engine is now consuming air from the manifold at a rate that balances the incoming airflow from the propeller.

In turbocharged engines, the manifold pressure gauge may indicate an increase in pressure during engine start as the turbocharger begins to spool up and compress air into the intake manifold. This increase is a result of the turbocharger's action and is necessary to provide the engine with a higher air density for combustion.

[PA.I.G, CA.I.G; FAA-H-8083-25]

13. Can the manifold pressure (inches of mercury) setting ever exceed propeller RPM for cruise power settings?

In a normally aspirated (non-turbocharged) aircraft engine, the manifold pressure (in inches of mercury, or inHg) setting is generally not set to exceed propeller RPM for cruise power settings. Manifold pressure represents the pressure of the air-fuel mixture in the engine's intake manifold, while propeller RPM indicates the rotational speed of the propeller.

During cruise power settings, the manifold pressure is typically set to achieve the desired power output for the given altitude and flight conditions. This setting corresponds to a specific throttle position that balances the engine's power requirements with the available air density.

On the other hand, propeller RPM is adjusted to optimize the propeller's efficiency and achieve the desired airspeed for cruise flight. The RPM setting is independent of the manifold pressure setting and is adjusted separately using the propeller control.

[PA.I.G, CA.I.G; FAA-H-8083-3]

14. What are several ways the pilot can control engine temperature?

Increase airspeed, enrich the mixture, and/or reduce power. On airplanes equipped with cowl flaps, use of different cowl flap positions can help in controlling engine temperature.

[PA.I.G, CA.I.G; FAA-H-8083-25]

15. What are cowl flaps?

Cowl flaps are hinged covers that fit over an opening in the engine cowling through which hot air is expelled. If the engine temperature is low, the cowl flaps can be closed, thereby restricting the flow of expelled hot air and increasing engine temperature. If the engine temperature is high, the cowl flaps can be opened to permit a greater flow of air through the system, thereby decreasing the engine temperature.

[PA.I.G, CA.I.G; FAA-H-8083-25]

16. What is an EGT probe?

The exhaust gas temperature (EGT) probe measures the temperature of the gases at the exhaust manifold and then transmits that information to an instrument in the flight deck. This temperature varies with the ratio of fuel to air entering the cylinders and can be used as a basis for regulating the air-fuel mixture.

[PA.I.G, CA.I.G; FAA-H-8083-25]

17. What is the correct procedure for leaning an engine with an EGT gauge (if applicable) and without?

Leaning an aircraft engine using exhaust gas temperature (EGT) involves adjusting the fuel mixture to achieve the most efficient air-fuel ratio for combustion, maximizing engine performance while minimizing fuel consumption.

In cruise flight, while monitoring the EGT gauge (potentially if equipped for each cylinder), the pilot will gradually lean the mixture control until the mixture reaches a peak EGT value. From there, the most common method is the "rich of peak" method in which the pilot will slightly enrichen the mixture to ensure adequate cooling and prevent potential engine damage due to excessively high temperatures. Some engines do allow a "lean of peak" process where specific parameters are designed to gain added fuel efficiency. If this method will be used, the pilot should carefully follow manufacturer recommendations to avoid doing engine damage.

[PA.I.G, CA.I.G; POH/AFM]

18. Explain the purpose and function of a turbocharger.

Turbochargers increase the pressure of the engine's induction air, which allows the engine to develop sea level or greater horsepower at higher altitudes. A turbocharger is comprised of two main elements: a compressor and a turbine.

Compressor—The compressor section houses an impeller that turns at a high rate of speed. As induction air is drawn across the impeller blades, it is accelerated, allowing a large volume of air to be drawn into the compressor housing. The impeller's action subsequently produces high-pressure, high-density air that is delivered to the engine.

Turbine—To turn the impeller, the engine's exhaust gases are used to drive a turbine wheel that is mounted on the opposite end of the impeller's drive shaft. By directing different amounts of exhaust gases to flow over the turbine, more energy can be extracted, causing the impeller to deliver more compressed air to the engine.

[PA.I.G, CA.I.G, CA.VII.A, CA.VIII.B; FAA-H-8083-25]

19. What is the name of the device that regulates the flow of exhaust gas to the turbine?

The waste gate controller. This is essentially an adjustable butterfly valve installed in the exhaust system and is used to vary the mass of exhaust gas flowing into the turbine. When closed, most of the exhaust gases from the engine are forced to flow through the turbine. When open, the exhaust gases are allowed to bypass the turbine by flowing directly out through the engine's exhaust pipe.

[PA.I.G, CA.I.G; FAA-H-8083-25]

20. If a pilot experiences a turbocharger failure while in flight, what would be expected to occur and how should the pilot handle it?

Because of the high temperatures and pressures produced in the turbine exhaust system, any malfunction of the turbocharger should be treated with extreme caution. In all cases of turbocharger operation, the manufacturer's recommended procedures should be followed. This is especially so in the case of turbocharger malfunction. However, in those instances where the manufacturer's procedures do not adequately describe the actions to be taken in the event of a turbocharger failure, the following procedures should be used.

Over-boost condition—If an excessive rise in manifold pressure occurs during normal advancement of the throttle (possibly owing to faulty operation of the waste gate): Immediately retard the throttle smoothly to limit the manifold pressure below the maximum for the RPM and mixture setting. Operate the engine in such a manner as to avoid a further over-boost condition.

Low manifold pressure—Although this condition may be caused by a minor fault, it is quite possible that a serious exhaust leak has occurred, creating a potentially hazardous situation. Shut down the engine in accordance with the recommended engine failure procedures, unless a greater emergency exists that warrants continued engine operation. If continuing to operate the engine, use the lowest power setting demanded by the situation and land as soon as practicable.

[PA.I.G, CA.I.G; FAA-H-8083-3]

21. Explain the purpose of an intercooler.

Since the temperature of a gas rises when it is compressed, turbocharging causes the temperature of the induction air to increase. To reduce this temperature and lower the risk of detonation, many turbocharged engines use an intercooler. This small heat exchanger uses outside air to cool the hot compressed air before it enters the fuel metering device.

[PA.I.G, CA.I.G; FAA-H-8083-25]

22. What is a constant-speed propeller?

A constant-speed propeller is a propeller whose pitch or blade angle is automatically varied in flight by a governor to maintain a constant RPM in spite of varying air loads. In many aircraft, these controls are manually adjusted, but in some more modern aircraft that are FADEC (full authority digital engine control), the controls may be incorporated into one throttle level and the adjustment is done automatically.

[PA.I.G, CA.I.G; FAA-H-8083-3]

23. What does the propeller governor do to blade angle when an airplane is nosed up into a climb from level flight, or nosed down into a descent?

As the airplane enters the climb, the engine will tend to slow down. Since the governor is sensitive to small changes in engine RPM, it will decrease the blade angle just enough to keep the engine speed from falling off. If the airplane is nosed down into a dive, the governor will increase the blade angle enough to prevent the engine from overspeeding. This allows the engine to maintain a constant RPM, and thus maintain the power output.

[PA.I.G, CA.I.G; FAA-H-8083-3]

24. How are the propellers on multi-engine airplanes different than almost all constant-speed propellers found on single-engine airplanes?

The propellers of multi-engine airplanes are featherable, to minimize drag in the event of an engine failure. Depending upon single-engine performance, this feature often permits continued flight to a suitable airport following an engine failure. In most single-engine aircraft, a loss of control of the propeller blade angle (most commonly a loss of hydraulic pressure in the propeller hub) will result in a movement of the blade angle to a low pitch, high RPM condition. In a multi-engine aircraft, the propeller will tend to move toward high relative pitch and low RPM settings, moving toward a feathered position to assist in the reduction of drag and/or V_{MC} encounter.

[PA.I.G, CA.I.G; FAA-H-8083-3]

25. Why is it necessary to "exercise" the propellers prior to takeoff?

This is done to determine whether the system is operating correctly and to circulate fresh, warm oil through the propeller governor system. This is an opportunity to see if there are any leaks in the system, if a proper exchange of oil is taking place in the propeller hub, and if the propeller returns to the high RPM condition appropriately when the propeller control lever is pushed back forward.

[PA.I.G, CA.I.G; FAA-H-8083-3]

26. What possible problem could occur on takeoff if the propellers are not exercised before takeoff?

If the propeller isn't exercised before takeoff, there is a possibility that the engine may overspeed on takeoff if the oil has been trapped in the propeller cylinder since the last time the engine was shut down. There is a certain amount of leakage from the propeller cylinder, and the oil tends to congeal, especially if the outside air temperature is low.

[PA.I.G, CA.I.G; FAA-H-8083-3]

27. What is a propeller overspeed?

A propeller overspeed is a condition in which the propeller speed is higher than the desired speed set on the propeller control. The usual cause is a malfunctioning propeller governor, which puts the propeller blades into a full low pitch, high RPM condition.

[PA.I.G, CA.I.G; AFM]

28. If a propeller overspeed occurs, what procedure should be followed?

Reference your aircraft's airplane flight manual (AFM). In general, your response should be to immediately reduce power and set the propeller control to a full "Decrease RPM" position. If necessary, increase the aircraft's pitch attitude to decrease airspeed.

[PA.I.G, CA.I.G; AFM]

29. What is accomplished when feathering a propeller?

When an engine propeller is "feathered," engine rotation is stopped and the propeller blades are streamlined with the airplane's relative wind, minimizing drag.

[PA.I.G, CA.I.G; FAA-H-8083-3]

30. Which direction do the blades move when increasing the oil pressure in the propeller hub in a multi-engine aircraft?

The constant-speed propellers installed on most multi-engine airplanes are full-feathering, counterweighted, oil-pressure-to-decrease-pitch designs. In this design, increased oil pressure from the propeller governor drives the blade angle toward low pitch, high RPM—away from the feather blade angle. In effect, the only thing that keeps these propellers from feathering is a constant supply of high-pressure engine oil. This is a necessity to enable propeller feathering in the event of a loss of oil pressure or a propeller governor failure.

[PA.I.G, CA.I.G; FAA-H-8083-3]

31. What is the purpose of counterweights on the propeller blades of some multi-engine aircraft?

Counterweights assist in driving the propeller blades towards feather. The aerodynamic forces alone, acting upon a windmilling propeller, tend to drive the blades to low pitch, high RPM. Counterweights attached to the shank of each blade tend to drive the blades to high pitch, low RPM. Inertia, or the apparent force called centrifugal force, acting through the counterweights, is generally slightly greater than the aerodynamic forces.

[PA.I.G, CA.I.G; FAA-H-8083-3]

32. Describe the procedure for feathering a propeller.

To feather the propeller, the propeller control is brought fully aft. All oil pressure is dumped from the governor, and the counterweights drive the propeller blades towards feather. As centrifugal force acting on the counterweights decays from decreasing RPM, additional forces are needed to completely feather the blades. This additional force comes from either a spring or high-pressure air stored in the propeller dome, which forces the blades into the feathered position. The entire process may take up to 10 seconds.

[PA.I.G, CA.I.G; FAA-H-8083-3]

33. How is a propeller brought out of the feathered position?

To unfeather a propeller, the engine must be rotated so that oil pressure can be generated to move the propeller blades from the feathered position. The ignition is turned on prior to engine rotation with the throttle at low idle and the mixture rich. With the propeller control in a high RPM position, the starter is engaged. The engine will begin to windmill, start, and run as oil pressure moves the blades out of feather.

[PA.I.G, CA.I.G; FAA-H-8083-3]

34. What is an unfeathering accumulator?

An unfeathering accumulator is an optional device that permits starting a feathered engine in flight without prolonged or potentially any use of the electric starter. The unfeathering accumulator stores a small reserve of engine oil under pressure from compressed air or nitrogen. To start a feathered engine in flight, the pilot moves the propeller control out of the feather position to release the accumulator pressure. The oil flows under pressure to the propeller hub and drives the blades toward the high RPM, low pitch position, and the propeller usually begins to windmill. If fuel and ignition are present, the engine will start and run.

[PA.I.G, CA.I.G; FAA-H-8083-3]

35. How are the propellers synchronized in flight?

Some multi-engine airplanes have a propeller synchronizer that is electrically actuated. To use prop sync, the propeller RPMs are coarsely matched by the pilot and the system is engaged. The prop sync adjusts the RPM of the "slave" engine to precisely match the RPM of the "master" engine, and then maintains that relationship. The prop sync should be disengaged when the pilot selects a new propeller RPM, then re-engaged after the new RPM is set. In the absence of such a system, syncing must be done manually.

[PA.I.G, CA.I.G; FAA-H-8083-3]

36. What is a propeller synchrophaser?

A prop synchrophaser acts much like a synchronizer to precisely match RPM, but the synchrophaser goes one step further. It not only matches RPM but actually compares and adjusts the positions of the individual blades of the propellers in their arcs. This can lead to significant reductions in propeller noise and vibration.

[PA.I.G, CA.I.G; FAA-H-8083-3]

37. How are the propellers synchronized in airplanes without a propeller synchronizer?

The propellers can be synchronized manually by setting one propeller (usually the left) to the desired RPM, then adjusting the other propeller RPM until the audible "drumming" or "beat" has slowed and then stopped. If equipped, digital RPM indications can help a pilot get more precise adjustments and assist in the syncing process.

[PA.I.G, CA.I.G; POH/AFM]

38. Why don't the propeller blades feather every time an engine is shut down as oil pressure falls to zero?

Most multi-engine aircraft are equipped with a "lockout pin" that stops the propeller from feathering when the engine is stopped. This small pin in the pitch-changing mechanism of the propeller hub prevents this from occurring by not allowing the propeller blades to feather once RPM drops below approximately 800. The pin senses a lack of centrifugal force from propeller rotation and falls into place, preventing the blades from feathering. This also means that if a propeller is to be feathered, it must be done before engine RPM decays below approximately 800.

[PA.I.G, CA.I.G; FAA-H-8083-3]

39. Describe how securing and shutting down an engine will affect the operation of the hydraulic, electrical, landing gear, vacuum, and/or flap systems.

Depending on the systems on a particular aircraft, shutting an engine down may affect systems other than just the engine itself. Most multi-engine aircraft have a generator or alternator on both engines. Shutting down an engine will take one of these offline and may reduce the available power for charging to the batteries if one engine and its corresponding generator/alternator is offline.

Frequently, modern twin-engine aircraft will have vacuum pumps and hydraulic pumps on both engines. These are redundant in the case of failure of one or the other, or either engine. In some older twin-engine aircraft, there may only be one hydraulic pump. If the gear system is hydraulically actuated and the failed engine is the one that has the hydraulic pump, it may become necessary for the pilot to execute an emergency gear extension due to lack of a functional hydraulic pump on the affected engine. In some cases, flaps may additionally be hydraulically actuated, and that system may also be affected.

Vacuum pumps when failed may also affect aircraft pressurization systems. If one pump has failed, it is possible that full pressurization ability may not be maintained and the pilot in a pressurized aircraft may need to descend.

[PA.I.G, CA.I.G; POH/AFM]

D. Landing Gear

1. **Explain the importance of the preflight inspection of the landing gear, including which items must be inspected, the reasons for checking each item, and how to detect possible defects.**

Inspection of the landing gear and its systems prior to flight can ensure that the components have not been damaged and are likely to work properly during the flight operation. Key points that should be included include an external inspection of shocks and struts, squat switches, any micro-switches that actuate warning indications, alignment of the gear, properly serviced tire pressures, clear actuator arms and retraction bay, and any seals to ensure they are not leaking. Internal inspection of gear actuator switches, position indications, and emergency operations controls should also be part of a good preflight. Refer closely to the manufacturer's AFM/POH to understand the components that a pilot can inspect prior to flight for safe operations.

[PA.II.A, CA.II.A; POH/AFM, FAA-H-8083-3]

2. Describe how an electric landing gear extension/ retraction system works.

This system uses an electrically driven motor for gear operation and is basically an electrically driven jack for raising and lowering the gear. When a switch in the flight deck is moved to the UP position, the electric motor operates. Through a system of shafts, gears, adapters, etc., a force is transmitted to the drag strut linkages and the gear retracts and locks. Struts are also activated that open and close the gear doors. If the switch is moved to the DOWN position, the motor reverses and the gear moves down and locks. Once activated, the gear motor will continue to operate until an up or down limit switch on the motor's gearbox is tripped.

[PA.I.G, CA.I.G; FAA-H-8083-3]

3. Describe how a hydraulic landing gear system works.

This system uses pressurized hydraulic fluid to actuate linkages to raise and lower the gear. When a switch in the flight deck is moved to the UP position, hydraulic fluid is directed into the gear up line. The fluid flows through sequenced valves and downlocks to the gear actuating cylinders. A similar process occurs during gear extension. The pump that pressurizes the fluid in the system can be either engine-driven or electrically powered. If an electrically powered pump is used to pressurize the fluid, the system is referred to as an electro-hydraulic system.

[PA.I.G, CA.I.G; FAA-H-8083-3]

4. What are hydraulic limit switches?

Limit switches regulate the hydraulic pressure; they de-energize the hydraulic pump after the landing gear has completed its gear cycle. In the event of limit switch failure, a backup pressure relief valve activates to relieve excess system pressure.

[PA.I.G, CA.I.G; FAA-H-8083-3]

5. What mechanism keeps the landing gear locked in the up position?

Some aircraft have uplocks; others use hydraulic pressure to keep the gear in the up and locked position.

[PA.I.G, CA.I.G; POH/AFM]

6. What conditions will cause the gear warning horn to sound?

The gear warning horn will sound when the airplane is configured for landing and the landing gear is not down and locked. Normally, the horn is linked to the throttle and/or flap position, and/or to the airspeed indicator, so that when the airplane is below a certain airspeed, configuration, or power setting with the gear retracted, the warning horn will sound. Knowing how these work serves as a good backup to the visual indications of aircraft gear down indications in the event of a failure of an indicator.

[PA.I.G, CA.I.G; FAA-H-8083-3]

7. How is inadvertent gear retraction on the ground prevented?

Accidental retraction of the landing gear may be prevented by such devices as mechanical downlocks, safety switches, and ground locks. Mechanical downlocks are built-in components of a gear retraction system and are operated automatically. To prevent accidental release of the downlocks and inadvertent landing gear retraction while the airplane is on the ground, electrically operated safety switches are installed.

[PA.I.G, CA.I.G; FAA-H-8083-3]

8. Explain how a landing gear safety switch (squat switch) operates.

A landing gear safety switch, sometimes referred to as a squat switch, is usually mounted in a bracket on one of the main gear shock struts. When the strut is compressed by the weight of the airplane, the switch opens the electrical circuit to the motor or mechanism that powers retraction. In this way, if the landing gear switch in the flight deck is placed in the RETRACT position when weight is on the gear, the gear will remain extended, and the warning horn may sound as an alert to the unsafe condition.

[PA.I.G, CA.I.G; FAA-H-8083-3]

9. **What are several types of ground locks used to prevent collapse of the gear on the ground?**

Gear pins are installed in aligned holes drilled in two or more units of the landing gear support structure. Another type is a spring-loaded clip designed to fit around and hold two or more units of the support structure together. All types of ground locks usually have red streamers permanently attached to them to readily indicate whether or not they are installed.

[PA.I.G, CA.I.G; FAA-H-8083-3]

10. **If the source of power for the landing gear system fails, how is emergency gear extension accomplished?**

Some airplanes have an emergency release handle in the flight deck, which is connected through a mechanical linkage to the gear uplocks. When the handle is operated, it releases the uplocks and allows the gear to free-fall, or extend under their own weight. On other airplanes, release of the uplock is accomplished using compressed gas, which is directed to uplock release cylinders. In some airplanes, design configurations make emergency extension of the landing gear by gravity and air loads alone impossible or impractical, so provisions are included for forceful gear extension in an emergency. Some installations are designed so that either hydraulic fluid or compressed gas provides the necessary pressure, while others use a manual system such as a hand crank for emergency gear extension. Hydraulic pressure for emergency operation of the landing gear may be provided by an auxiliary hand pump, an accumulator, or an electrically powered hydraulic pump, depending on the design of the airplane.

Note: Know what emergency gear extension options are available and how they work in your aircraft. It will also be important to know if their operation can be simulated without causing any systems damage or requiring additional assistance from maintenance staff if an emergency gear extension has been conducted.

[PA.I.G, CA.I.G; FAA-H-8083-3]

11. How is the landing gear position indicated in the flight deck?

One type of indicator consists of a group of three green lights that illuminate when the landing gear is down and locked. Another type consists of one green light to indicate when the landing gear is down and an amber light to indicate when the gear is up. Still other systems incorporate a red or amber light to indicate when the gear is in transit or unsafe for landing. A few aircraft have additional visual indicators, such as down on the floor, and many modern aircraft have incorporated the gear down indications into digital PFD/MFD displays.

[PA.I.G, CA.I.G; FAA-H-8083-3]

12. If one or more landing gear indicator lights have not illuminated, and you are reasonably sure the gear has extended and locked, what initial action should be taken?

This situation could be the result of a burned-out bulb. A quick check can be made by using the "press-to-test" feature incorporated into the bulb (if applicable). If the bulb is burned out, or you are still uncertain as to the gear status, a known operative bulb can be used (swapping). Also, on some aircraft, when the navigation lights are switched on, the landing gear indicator lights will automatically dim (and may be difficult to see during daytime). A backup indication that can be used is to retard throttle or deploy flaps to see if an audible gear warning horn is engaged. If a light is out but the pilot does not get a gear warning horn when these other systems are engaged, it is typically an indication that the gear may be down and locked and it may just be an indicator problem.

[PA.I.G, CA.I.G; POH/AFM]

13. What indications, other than the indicator lights, assist in detection of fully extended or retracted landing gear?

As the landing gear extends or retracts, airspeed will change, and the airplane's pitch attitude may change. The gear may take several seconds to extend or retract. Gear extension, retraction, and locking is accompanied by sound and feel that are unique to the specific make and model airplane. The pilot should become familiar with the sounds and feel of normal gear extension, retraction, and locking so that any abnormal gear operation can be readily discernable. Abnormal landing gear retraction is most often a clear sign that the gear extension cycle will also be abnormal.

[PA.I.G, CA.I.G; FAA-H-8083-3]

14. If the landing gear is hydraulically actuated, what problems would you have in the event of an engine failure on departure, before retracting the landing gear?

If the airplane's landing gear retraction mechanism is dependent upon hydraulic pressure from a certain engine-driven pump, failure of that engine can mean a loss of hundreds of feet of altitude as the pilot either windmills the engine to provide hydraulic pressure to raise the gear or raises it manually with a backup pump.

Note: Some multi-engine aircraft have multiple hydraulic pumps, while some have only one. In an aircraft where only one hydraulic pump is present, a failure of the engine that has the pump may additionally require the pilot to manually extend the gear.

[PA.I.G, CA.I.G; FAA-H-8083-3]

15. Describe the difference between V_{LE} and V_{LO}.

V_{LE} is the maximum airspeed at which the airplane can be safely flown with the landing gear extended. This is a problem involving stability and controllability.

V_{LO} is the maximum airspeed at which the landing gear can be safely extended or retracted. This is a problem involving the air loads imposed on the operating mechanism (gear doors, etc.) during extension or retraction of the gear.

[PA.I.F, CA.I.F; FAA-H-8083-25]

E. Fuel, Oil, and Hydraulic

Exam Tip: Be prepared to provide and explain a diagram of the fuel system in your airplane. This is a common weak area on the practical test.

1. What grade of fuel is used in your airplane?

The proper fuel grade is stated in the AFM or POH, on placards in the flight deck, and next to the filler caps. Most light general aviation aircraft used in training use 100LL Avgas. Some modern piston aircraft are capable of using Jet A fuel, and most turbine aircraft use Jet A fuel. Be sure to know what fuel is appropriate for the aircraft you will be using. Also be aware if your aircraft engines are capable of using sustainable aviation fuels (SAF).

[PA.I.G, CA.I.G; POH/AFM]

2. What are the locations of the aircraft fuel tanks and what are their capacities (total and usable)?

The location and capacities of fuel tanks vary with each aircraft. Multi-engine airplanes may have multiple fuel tank locations with tanks located in the inboard and outboard sections of the wings and, in larger multi-engine aircraft, in the fuselage. Be sure to know if there are specific tanks that must be selected during takeoff and landing, if there are limitations on some tanks that must only be used during straight-and-level (cruising) flight, or if tanks pump fuel directly to engine usage or pump into another fuel tank.

[PA.I.G, CA.I.G; POH/AFM]

3. How are the fuel tanks vented to the outside atmosphere?

Fuel tanks may be vented through the filler cap or through a tube extending through the surface of the wing, or both.

[PA.I.G, CA.I.G; POH/AFM]

4. Where are the fuel tank overflow drain(s) on the aircraft, and why are they needed?

Fuel tanks usually include an overflow drain that may stand alone or be co-located with the fuel tank vent. It allows fuel to expand with increases in temperature without damage to the tank itself. If the tanks have been filled on a hot day, it is not unusual to see fuel coming from the overflow drain.

[PA.I.G, CA.I.G; POH/AFM]

5. How does the fuel system provide fuel to the engines on the aircraft?

The fuel system may allow fuel to travel to the engines either via a gravity-fed system or through the use of mechanical and/or electric fuel pump types of systems. Many aircraft will have mechanical engine-driven fuel pumps that are supplemented for priming or backup by electrically driven pumps.

[PA.I.G, CA.I.G; POH/AFM]

6. How many fuel pumps are used in the aircraft fuel system?

Airplanes with fuel pump systems have two fuel pumps per engine. The main pump system is engine-driven, and an electrically driven auxiliary pump is provided for use in engine starting and in the event the engine pump fails. The auxiliary pump, also known as a boost pump, provides added reliability to the fuel system. The electrically driven auxiliary pump is controlled by a switch in the flight deck. These auxiliary pumps are not always able to provide sufficient fuel pressure for the engines to be run at full power.

[PA.I.G, CA.I.G; POH/AFM]

7. What is the function of the fuel strainers, sumps, and drains on the airplane?

Fuel strainers remove moisture and other sediments that might be in the system. Since these contaminants are heavier than aviation fuel, they settle in a sump at the bottom of the strainer assembly. A sump is defined as a low point in a fuel system and/or fuel tank. Fuel systems may contain sumps, fuel strainers, and fuel tank drains, some of which may be co-located.

[PA.I.G, CA.I.G; FAA-H-8083-25]

8. Describe how a fuel primer system works.

A fuel primer is used to draw fuel from the tanks to vaporize it directly into the cylinders prior to starting the engine. This is particularly helpful during cold weather, when engines are hard to start because there is not enough heat available to vaporize the fuel in the carburetor.

[PA.I.G, CA.I.G; FAA-H-8083-25]

9. How does the condition known as vapor lock occur in a fuel system?

Vapor lock is a condition in which air enters the fuel system, making it difficult or even impossible to restart the engine. Vapor lock may occur as a result of running a fuel tank completely dry, allowing air to enter the fuel system. On fuel-injected engines, the fuel may become so hot it vaporizes in the fuel line, not allowing fuel to reach the cylinders. A good practice is to understand and be able to complete a "hot start" procedure if this is suspected.

[PA.I.G, CA.I.G; FAA-H-8083-3]

10. What are the positions on the fuel selector valves in the airplane?

A three-position fuel selector valve for each engine is common, with the positions "ON," "OFF," and "X-FEED."

[PA.I.G, CA.I.G; POH/AFM]

11. What is the primary reason for a fuel crossfeed system in a multi-engine fuel system?

On most multi-engine airplanes, operation in the crossfeed mode is an emergency procedure used to extend airplane range and endurance in one engine inoperative flight. Some models of aircraft permit crossfeed as a normal, fuel balancing technique in normal operation, but these are less common. The POH/AFM will describe crossfeed limitations and procedures, which vary significantly among multi-engine airplanes. Crossfeed might additionally be used if an engine is running poorly and fuel contamination is suspected.

Important: Have a thorough understanding of the procedure for crossfeed operations in your airplane.

[PA.I.G, CA.I.G; FAA-H-8083-3]

12. What does a quick repositioning of the fuel selector valve on the ground accomplish?

Repositioning of the fuel selectors on the ground does nothing more than ensure freedom of motion of the handle. To actually check crossfeed operation, a complete, functional crossfeed system check should be accomplished.

[PA.II.F, CA.II.F; FAA-H-8083-3]

13. How would a complete and functional crossfeed check be performed?

A complete crossfeed check would allow each engine to be operated from its crossfeed position during the run-up. The engines should be checked individually and be allowed to run at moderate power (1,500 RPM minimum) for at least 1 minute to ensure that fuel flow can be established from the crossfeed source. Upon completion of the check, each engine should be operated for at least 1 minute at moderate power from the main (takeoff) fuel tanks to reconfirm fuel flow prior to takeoff.

[PA.II.F, CA.II.F; FAA-H-8083-3]

14. How often should the fuel crossfeed system be checked?

This suggested check is usually not required prior to every flight. Infrequently used, however, crossfeed lines are ideal places for water and debris to accumulate unless they are used from time to time and drained using their external drains during preflight.

[PA.II.F, CA.II.F; FAA-H-8083-3]

15. How is fuel quantity measured and indicated?

Fuel quantity gauges indicate the amount of fuel measured by a sensing unit in each fuel tank and the quantity is displayed in gallons or pounds. Many older aircraft have float-type fuel gauges that translate to analog fuel indicators. Newer, more modern aircraft may have digital sensors that report more accurately. In any aircraft, visual verification of fuel quantity should always be conducted and compared with gauge indications.

[PA.I.G, CA.I.G; POH/AFM]

16. Describe how a fuel vapor return system works.

In aircraft, fuel vapor return systems are essential components that manage and recycle fuel vapors to enhance safety, efficiency, and environmental performance. Unlike automotive systems, aircraft fuel vapor return systems are primarily designed to prevent fuel tank over-pressurization and reduce the risk of fuel vapor accumulation, which can pose safety hazards.

Aircraft fuel tanks are vented to allow air to enter and exit the tanks as fuel is consumed or as ambient temperature changes. These vents prevent the formation of a vacuum or excessive pressure inside the tanks, which could impede fuel flow or cause tank deformation.

As fuel is consumed and the aircraft operates, fuel vapors are generated within the fuel tanks due to changes in temperature, atmospheric pressure, and fuel movement. These vapors need to be managed to prevent them from accumulating and potentially creating a flammable atmosphere inside the tanks.

The fuel vapor return system typically includes a vapor return line that collects excess fuel vapors from the fuel tanks. This line is connected to each fuel tank and may incorporate check valves or other mechanisms to prevent the backflow of fuel or vapors.

[PA.I.G, CA.I.G; POH/AFM]

17. The engine oil system performs several important functions. What are they?

a. Lubrication of the engine's moving parts.

b. Cooling of the engine by reducing friction.

c. Removing heat from the cylinders.

d. Providing a seal between the cylinder walls and pistons.

e. Carrying away contaminants.

[PA.I.G, CA.I.G; FAA-H-8083-25]

18. What is the difference between a wet-sump and dry-sump oil system?

In a dry-sump system, the oil is contained in a separate tank and circulated through the engine by pumps. In a wet-sump system, the oil is located in a sump which is an integral part of the engine.

[PA.I.G, CA.I.G; FAA-H-8083-25]

19. Does the oil temperature gauge give a direct indication of engine temperature?

No. The oil temperature gauge gives only an indirect and delayed indication of rising engine temperature, but it can be used for determining engine temperature if this is the only means available. If available, a cylinder-head temperature gauge will give the most direct and immediate indication of cylinder temperature range.

[PA.I.G, CA.I.G; FAA-H-8083-25]

20. What possible problems could cause an oil temperature gauge to indicate very high or low temperatures?

High temperature indications may indicate a plugged oil line, a low oil quantity, a blocked oil cooler, or a defective temperature gauge. Low temperature indications may indicate improper oil viscosity during cold weather operations.

[PA.I.G, CA.I.G; FAA-H-8083-25]

21. What are the components of a basic hydraulic system?

A hydraulic system consists of a reservoir, a pump (either hand, electric, or engine driven), a filter to keep the fluid clean, a selector valve to control the direction of flow, a relief valve to relieve excess pressure, and an actuator.

[PA.I.G, CA.I.G; FAA-H-8083-25]

22. What is a servo?

A servo is a cylinder with a piston inside that turns fluid power into work and creates the power needed to move an aircraft system or flight control.

[PA.I.G, CA.I.G; FAA-H-8083-25]

23. Describe how a basic hydraulic system works.

Hydraulic fluid is pumped through the system to an actuator or a single-acting/double-acting servo based on the needs of the system. Fluid can be applied in one direction with a single-acting servo and in both directions with a double-acting servo. A selector valve allows the fluid direction to be controlled. This is necessary for operations like the extension and retraction of landing gear where the fluid must work in two different directions. A relief valve provides an outlet for the system in the event of excessive fluid pressure in the system.

[PA.I.G, CA.I.G; FAA-H-8083-25]

24. What type of hydraulic fluid does your aircraft use, and what is its color?

Refer to your POH/AFM. A mineral-based hydraulic fluid (MIL-H-5606) is the most widely used type for small aircraft. It has an odor similar to penetrating oil and is dyed red. A newer, fire-resistant fluid (MIL-H-83282) is also used in small aircraft and is dyed red.

[PA.I.G, CA.I.G; FAA-H-8083-25; FAA-H-8083-31]

25. What systems are operated based on a hydraulic system in multi-engine aircraft?

While not all aircraft have hydraulic systems, some aircraft have hydraulic systems that operate landing gear, and a few have hydraulic flap systems. Understand how these systems operate and the failure modes on your particular aircraft, if it is equipped with such systems.

[PA.I.G, CA.I.G; FAA-H-8083-25, POH/AFM]

F. Electrical

1. Describe the main difference between an alternator and a generator.

Most direct current generators will not produce a sufficient amount of electrical current at low engine RPM to operate the entire electrical system. During operations at low engine RPM, the electrical needs must be drawn from the battery, which can quickly be depleted. Alternators produce sufficient current to operate the entire electrical system, even at slower engine speeds, by producing alternating current, which is converted to direct current.

The electrical output of an alternator is more constant throughout a wide range of engine speeds.

[PA.I.G, CA.I.G; FAA-H-8083-25]

2. What is the purpose of alternator/generator paralleling circuitry in multi-engine aircraft?

Alternator or generator paralleling circuitry matches the output of each engine's alternator/generator so that the electrical system load is shared equally between them.

[PA.I.G, CA.I.G; FAA-H-8083-3]

3. What is meant by the term *load shedding*?

Depending upon the electrical capacity of the alternator/generator, the pilot may need to reduce the electrical load (referred to as load shedding) when operating on a single unit. The POH/AFM will contain system descriptions and limitations.

[PA.I.G, CA.I.G; FAA-H-8083-3]

4. If one alternator/generator fails, can the remaining alternator/generator power the electrical system?

Normally, the inoperative unit can be isolated, and the electrical system can then be powered by the remaining alternator/generator. It may be necessary for the pilot to "load shed" if the power draw is greater than a single alternator/generator is able to support. Common items that the pilot might consider turning off in the load-shedding effort might be backup radios, interior or even potentially external lights that are not needed, and/or deicing equipment if not needed. A pilot can manage this effort by monitoring electrical draw indications.

[PA.I.G, CA.I.G; FAA-H-8083-3]

5. How are the electrical circuits protected in the aircraft?

Fuses or circuit breakers are used in the electrical system to protect the circuits and equipment from electrical overload. Circuit breakers have the same function as a fuse but can be manually reset, rather than replaced, if an overload condition occurs in the electrical system. Placards at the fuse or circuit breaker panel identify the circuit by name and show the amperage limit.

[PA.I.G, CA.I.G; FAA-H-8083-25]

6. What procedure is recommended when resetting a tripped circuit breaker?

A tripped circuit breaker should not be reset in flight unless doing so is consistent with procedures specified in an approved AFM, or unless, in the judgment of the PIC, resetting the breaker is necessary for safe completion of the flight. Repeated resetting of a circuit breaker can lead to circuit or component damage—or worse, the possibility of a fire or explosion.

[PA.I.G, CA.I.G; FAA-H-8083-30, AC 120-80]

7. What information does an ammeter provide?

An ammeter is used to monitor the performance of the aircraft electrical system. The ammeter shows if the alternator/generator is producing an adequate supply of electrical power. It also indicates whether or not the battery is receiving an electrical charge. Ammeters are designed with the zero point in the center of the face and a negative or positive indication on either side. When the pointer of the ammeter is on the plus side, it shows the charging rate of the battery. A minus indication means more current is being drawn from the battery than is being replaced. A full-scale minus deflection indicates a malfunction of the alternator/generator. A full-scale positive deflection indicates a malfunction of the regulator.

[PA.I.G, CA.I.G; FAA-H-8083-25]

8. What information does a loadmeter provide?

A loadmeter has a scale beginning with zero and shows the load being placed on the alternator/generator. It reflects the total percentage of the load placed on the generating capacity of the electrical system by the electrical accessories and battery. When all electrical components are turned off, it reflects only the amount of charging current demanded by the battery.

[PA.I.G, CA.I.G; FAA-H-8083-25]

9. What is the purpose of a voltage regulator?

A voltage regulator controls the rate of charge to the battery by stabilizing the generator or alternator electrical output. The generator/alternator voltage output should be higher than the battery voltage. For example, a 12-volt battery would be fed by a generator/alternator system of approximately 14 volts. The difference in voltage keeps the battery charged.

[PA.I.G, CA.I.G; FAA-H-8083-25]

10. What is an electrical bus bar?

An electrical bus bar is an electrical power distribution point to which several circuits may be connected. It is often a solid metal strip having a number of terminals installed on it.

[PA.I.G, CA.I.G; FAA-H-8083-3]

11. What is an electrical bus tie?

It is a switch that connects two or more bus bars. It is usually used when one generator fails and power is lost to its bus. By closing the switch, the operating generator powers both buses.

[PA.I.G, CA.I.G; FAA-H-8083-3]

G. Avionics

1. Describe the function of the following avionics equipment acronyms: AHRS, ADC, PFD, MFD, FD, FMS, and TAWS.

AHRS—Attitude and heading reference system. Composed of three-axis sensors that provide heading, attitude, and yaw information for aircraft. An AHRS is designed to replace traditional mechanical gyroscopic flight instruments and provide superior reliability and accuracy.

ADC—Air data computer. An aircraft computer that receives and processes pitot pressure, static pressure, and temperature to calculate very precise altitude, indicated airspeed, true airspeed, vertical speed, and air temperature.

PFD—Primary flight display. A display that provides increased situational awareness to the pilot by replacing the traditional six instruments with an easy-to-scan display that provides the horizon, airspeed, altitude, vertical speed, trend, trim, and rate of turn among other key relevant indications.

MFD—Multi-function display. A flight deck display capable of presenting information (navigation data, moving maps, terrain awareness, etc.) to the pilot in numerous configurable ways, often used in concert with the PFD.

FD—Flight director. An electronic flight computer that analyzes the navigation selections, signals, and aircraft parameters. It presents steering instructions on the flight display as command bars or crossbars for the pilot to position the nose of the aircraft over or follow.

FMS—Flight management system. A computer system containing a database to allow programming of routes, approaches, and departures that can supply navigation data to the flight director/ autopilot from various sources, and can calculate flight data such as fuel consumption, time remaining, possible range, and other values.

TAWS—Terrain awareness and warning system. Uses the aircraft's GPS navigation signal and altimetry systems to compare the position and trajectory of the aircraft against a more detailed terrain and obstacle database. This database attempts to detail every obstruction that could pose a threat to an aircraft in flight.

[PA.I.G, CA.I.G; FAA-H-8083-16]

2. What is the function of a magnetometer?

A magnetometer is a device that measures the strength of the Earth's magnetic field to determine aircraft heading. The magnetometer provides this information digitally to the AHRS, which then sends it to the PFD.

[PA.I.G, CA.I.G; FAA-H-8083-16]

3. When powering-up an aircraft with a FMS/RNAV unit installed, how will you verify the effective dates of the navigation database?

The effective dates for the navigation database are typically shown on a start-up screen that is displayed as the system cycles through its startup self-test.

[PA.I.G, CA.I.G; FAA-H-8083-16]

4. Does an aircraft have to remain stationary during AHRS system initialization?

Some AHRSs must be initialized on the ground prior to departure. The initialization procedure allows the system to establish a reference attitude used as a benchmark for all future attitude changes. Other systems are capable of initialization while taxiing as well as in flight.

[PA.I.G, CA.I.G; FAA-H-8083-16]

5. Which standby flight instruments are normally provided in an advanced avionics aircraft?

Every aircraft equipped with electronic flight instruments must also contain a minimal set of backup/standby instruments. Usually conventional round-dial instruments, they typically include an attitude indicator, an airspeed indicator, and an altimeter.

[PA.I.G, CA.I.G; FAA-H-8083-16]

6. If one display fails (PFD or MFD), what information will be presented on the remaining display?

In the event of a display failure, some systems offer a reversion capability to display the primary flight instruments and engine instruments on the remaining operative display.

[PA.I.G, CA.I.G; FAA-H-8083-16]

7. When a display failure occurs, what other system components will be affected?

In some systems, failure of a display will also result in partial loss of navigation, communication, and GPS capability. Refer to your specific POH/AFM.

[PA.I.G, CA.I.G; POH/AFM]

8. What display information will be affected when an ADC failure occurs?

Inoperative airspeed, altitude, and vertical speed indicators (red Xs) on the PFD indicate the failure of the air data computer.

[PA.I.G, CA.I.G; FAA-H-8083-16]

9. What display information will be lost when an AHRS failure occurs?

An inoperative attitude indicator (red X) on a PFD indicates failure of the AHRS.

[PA.I.G, CA.I.G; FAA-H-8083-16]

10. How will loss of a magnetometer affect the AHRS operation?

Heading information will be lost.

[PA.I.G, CA.I.G; FAA-H-8083-16]

11. For aircraft with electronic flight instrumentation, what is the function of the standby battery?

The standby battery is held in reserve and kept charged in case of a failure of the charging system and a subsequent exhaustion of the main battery. The standby battery is brought online when the main battery voltage is depleted to a specific value, approximately 19 volts. Generally, the standby battery switch must be in the ARM position for this to occur, but pilots should refer to the POH/AFM for specifics on their aircraft's electrical system.

[PA.I.G, CA.I.G; FAA-H-8083-15]

12. Give a brief description of a typical autopilot system.

An autopilot is a mechanical means to control an aircraft using electrical, hydraulic, or digital systems. It provides one, two, or three axis control of the aircraft (roll, pitch, and yaw). Some systems control only the ailerons (one axis), while others control ailerons and elevators or rudder (two axis). A three-axis autopilot controls the aircraft about the longitudinal, lateral, and vertical axes; and three different servos actuate the ailerons, the elevator, and the rudder.

[PA.I.G, CA.I.G; FAA-H-8083-15, FAA-H-8083-31]

13. What are the basic components of an autopilot system?

All autopilot systems contain the same basic components:

a. *Gyros*—to sense what the airplane is doing.

b. *Servos*—to move the control surfaces.

c. *Amplifier*—to increase the strength of the gyro signals enough to operate the servos.

d. A controller is also provided to allow manual control of the aircraft through the autopilot system.

[PA.I.G, CA.I.G; FAA-H-8083-31]

14. What is meant by the terms *rate-based* and *position-based* autopilot systems?

A *position-based autopilot* uses the attitude gyro to sense the degree of difference from a position such as wings level, a change in pitch, or a heading change. *Rate-based systems* use the turn-and-bank sensor for the autopilot system. The autopilot uses rate information on two of the aircraft's three axes: movement about the vertical axis (heading change or yaw) and about the longitudinal axis (roll).

[PA.I.G, CA.I.G; FAA-H-8083-15]

15. What are some of the basic features of an autopilot system?

The most common features available on autopilots are altitude and heading hold. More advanced systems may include a vertical speed and/or indicated airspeed hold mode. Most autopilot systems are also capable of tracking navigational aids.

[PA.I.G, CA.I.G; FAA-H-8083-25]

16. What aircraft system failure would cause the autopilot to operate erratically?

In some systems, a pneumatic system failure would cause the attitude/heading indicator gyros to spin down. As they spin down, they may wander, and if they are connected to the autopilot and/or flight director, this would cause incorrect movement or erroneous indications.

[PA.I.G, CA.I.G; FAA-H-8083-25]

17. In the event of an autopilot malfunction, how is an autopilot system disabled?

Autopilot systems normally incorporate a disconnect safety feature to automatically or manually disengage the system. Because autopilot systems differ widely in their operation, refer to the autopilot operating instructions in the AFM or POH.

[PA.I.G, CA.I.G; FAA-H-8083-25]

18. Is it possible to manually overpower the autopilot?

Most autopilot systems can be manually overridden. Refer to the POH/AFM.

[PA.I.G, CA.I.G; FAA-H-8083-25]

19. Will the autopilot allow the aircraft to stall if the pilot has selected a pitch attitude or climb rate that would result in exceedance of the critical angle of attack?

Many modern autopilot systems have envelope protection systems built into them. If engaged and equipped, such an autopilot will reduce the angle of attack to avoid allowing the aircraft to encounter a stall, even if the pilot has selected a climb rate or attitude that would exceed the critical angle of attack. It is important for the pilot to know if the particular autopilot system is capable of doing this, and if so, whether the function is enabled or disabled. In some cases, the pilot may choose to disable such an envelope protection system for the purpose of demonstrating required maneuvers.

[PA.I.G, CA.I.G; AFM/POH/Supplements]

20. Can the autopilot be used in the event of a single-engine emergency?

Most systems prohibit use of the autopilot for single-engine operations. Refer to the POH/AFM.

[PA.I.G, CA.I.G; POH/AFM]

21. What is a yaw damper?

The yaw damper is a servo that moves the rudder in response to inputs from a gyroscope or accelerometer that detects yaw rate. The yaw damper minimizes motion about the vertical axis caused by turbulence. The yaw damper should be off for takeoff and landing. There may be additional restrictions against its use during single-engine operation. Most yaw dampers can be engaged independently of the autopilot.

[PA.I.G, CA.I.G; FAA-H-8083-3]

H. Pitot-Static, Vacuum/Pressure, and Associated Flight Instruments

1. Describe the pitot-static system.

The pitot-static system consists of two major parts: the impact pressure chamber and lines, and the static pressure chamber and lines.

[PA.I.G, CA.I.G; FAA-H-8083-25]

2. Which instruments are connected to the pitot-static system?

The altimeter, the vertical speed indicator (vertical velocity indicator), and the airspeed indicator.

[PA.I.G, CA.I.G; FAA-H-8083-25]

3. Is there ice protection for the pitot tube?

Some airplanes may be equipped with pitot heat for flight in visible moisture. Consult the AFM for specific procedures regarding the use of pitot heat.

[PA.I.G, CA.I.G; FAA-H-8083-25]

4. How does the airspeed indicator work?

The airspeed indicator is a sensitive, differential pressure gauge which measures and shows promptly the difference between pitot or impact pressure and static pressure, the undisturbed atmospheric pressure at level flight. This difference in pressure is registered by the airspeed pointer on the face of the instrument, which is calibrated in miles per hour, knots, or both.

[PA.I.G, CA.I.G; FAA-H-8083-25]

5. Where are the static ports located on the aircraft?

Static pressure is usually sampled at one or more locations outside the aircraft. On some aircraft, air is sampled by static ports on the side of the electrically heated pitot-static head. Other aircraft pick up the static pressure through flush ports on the side of the fuselage or the vertical fin. The dual locations prevent lateral movement of the aircraft from giving erroneous static pressure indications. Be aware whether the static port on your aircraft is heated for de-icing efforts; it is not on all aircraft.

[PA.I.G, CA.I.G; FAA-H-8083-15]

6. What is the source of alternate static air?

In non-pressurized airplanes, most alternate static sources are plumbed to the cabin. On pressurized airplanes, they are usually plumbed to a non-pressurized baggage compartment. The pilot must activate the alternate static source by opening a valve or a fitting in the flight deck. If the alternate static air source is inside the cabin in a pressurized aircraft, in order to be used and have correct indications it may be necessary to de-pressurize the aircraft (and descend to a safe altitude for non-pressurized operations).

[PA.I.G, CA.I.G; FAA-H-8083-3]

7. What instrument indications should a pilot expect to see when using alternate air?

Reference your POH/AFM for details; however, there are some most common effects. When the alternate static source is vented inside the airplane; this static pressure is usually lower than the static pressure sensed from the outside static port. Therefore, selection of the alternate static source may result in the altimeter indicating higher than actual altitude, the airspeed indicator indicating greater than actual airspeed, and the vertical speed indicator momentarily indicating a climb while in level flight.

[PA.I.G, CA.I.G; FAA-H-8083-25, POH/AFM]

8. Explain how an altimeter measures altitude.

A sensitive altimeter is an aneroid barometer that measures the absolute pressure of the ambient air and displays it in terms of feet above a selected pressure level. The sensitive element in a sensitive altimeter is a stack of evacuated, corrugated bronze aneroid capsules. The air pressure acting on these aneroids tries to compress them against their natural springiness, which tries to expand them. The result is that their thickness changes as the air pressure changes. Stacking several aneroids increases the dimension change as the pressure varies over the usable range of the instrument.

[PA.I.G, CA.I.G; FAA-H-8083-15]

9. How does the vertical speed indicator work?

In the vertical speed indicator (VSI), changing pressures expand or contract a diaphragm connected to the indicating needle through gears and levers. The inside of the diaphragm is connected directly to the static line of the pitot-static system. The area outside the diaphragm, which is inside the instrument case, is also connected to the static line but through a restricted orifice (calibrated leak). The VSI measures this pressure differential as the airplane climbs or descends.

[PA.I.G, CA.I.G; FAA-H-8083-25]

10. Which flight instruments contain gyroscopes?

The most common gyroscopically driven instruments have historically been attitude indicators and heading indicators. Some turn coordinators may also be gyroscopic. Many modern aircraft no longer have vacuum-driven gyroscopic instruments, and a pilot should know which systems are in the aircraft they will be operating.

[PA.I.G, CA.I.G; FAA-H-8083-25]

11. Name several types of power sources commonly used to power the gyroscopic instruments in an aircraft.

Various power systems are used including vacuum, pressure, and electrically driven systems. Aircraft and instrument manufacturers have designed redundancy in the flight instruments so that any single failure will not deprive the pilot of the ability to safely conclude the flight. Gyroscopic instruments are crucial for instrument flight; therefore, they are powered by separate electrical or pneumatic sources.

Note: A vacuum system usually provides the power for the heading and attitude indicators, while the electrical system provides the power for the turn coordinator.

[PA.I.G, CA.I.G; FAA-H-8083-15]

12. How does a vacuum system operate?

The vacuum system spins a gyro within each instrument by drawing a stream of air against the rotor vane to spin the rotor at high speed, much like the operation of a waterwheel or turbine. The amount of vacuum required for instrument operation varies, but it is usually between 4.5 and 5.5 inHg. One source of vacuum for the gyros is a vane-type, engine-driven pump that is mounted on the accessory case of the engine.

[PA.I.G, CA.I.G; FAA-H-8083-25]

13. How is a vacuum pump failure indicated in the flight deck?

A vacuum or suction gauge is generally provided and is marked to indicate the normal range. Some airplanes are equipped with a warning light that illuminates when the vacuum pressure drops below the acceptable level.

[PA.I.G, CA.I.G; FAA-H-8083-25]

14. How does a pressure system operate?

Two dry air pumps are used with filters in their inlet to filter out contaminants. The discharge air from the pump flows through a regulator, where excess air is bled off to maintain the pressure in the system at the desired level. The regulated air then flows through inline filters to remove any contamination and from there, into a manifold check valve. After the air passes through the instruments and drives the gyros, it is exhausted from the case. The gyro pressure gauge measures the pressure drop across the instruments.

[PA.I.G, CA.I.G; FAA-H-8083-15]

15. In the event of a vacuum/pressure pump failure (internal failure, engine failure), is manual selection of the operative pump required?

Normally, if either engine should become inoperative or either pump should fail, a check valve isolates the inoperative system, and the instruments are driven by air from the operating system.

[PA.I.G, CA.I.G; FAA-H-8083-15]

I. Environmental

1. Explain the cabin ventilation system.

Ventilation air is obtained through ram air ducts installed in the leading, lower, or upper surfaces of the aircraft or through other vents in the aircraft skin. Air entering these openings usually passes into and through the same duct system that is used for heating and cooling. On some aircraft, recirculating fans or blowers are present in the system to assist in circulating the air.

[PA.I.G, CA.I.G; FAA-H-8083-31]

2. How does the cabin heating system operate?

Ram or blower ventilating air enters at the burner-head end of the heater and, passing over the heated radiator surfaces, becomes heated and passes through the outlet end into the plenum assembly and into the distribution system ductwork.

Many multi-engine aircraft have fuel-fired heater systems that provide direct heating to the aircraft; these are more complex than shroud-style heater systems in lighter single-engine aircraft that are used in aviation training or general aviation. Having systems such as this offers more heating potential for larger cabins that are found on larger and multi-engine aircraft.

These heater systems will commonly have overtemp or overheat protection systems. A pilot flying an aircraft equipped with these types of heater systems should understand how they are fired, their failure modes, what happens if they overtemp or catch fire, and how to cut fuel from them in the event that a heater system fire occurs.

[PA.I.G, CA.I.G; FAA-H-8083-31]

3. How is the cabin temperature controlled?

A cabin air temperature control knob adjusts a thermostat that controls the temperature in a duct located aft of the heater. When the temperature of the air exceeds the thermostat setting, the thermostat shuts down the heater. When the air temperature equals the thermostat setting, the heater is reactivated.

[PA.I.G, CA.I.G; FAA-H-8083-31]

4. What is a combustion heater?

It is a small furnace that burns gasoline to produce heated air for occupant comfort and windshield defogging. Most combustion heaters are thermostatically operated and have a separate hour meter to record time in service for maintenance purposes.

[PA.I.G, CA.I.G; FAA-H-8083-3]

5. If your aircraft is equipped with a combustion heater, where does it receive its fuel from and how much fuel is used per hour?

Fuel-fired heaters in aircraft are usually supplied from the same fuel system as the engines. Typically, the fuel will be from one specific tank and supplied either by gravity or pumped there by a fuel pump at a rate of approximately 0.5–1 gallon per hour. A pilot should consult the POH/AFM to determine from what tank and at what rate the fuel is supplied in their particular aircraft.

[PA.I.G, CA.I.G; FAA-H-8083-31]

6. When the combustion heater is no longer needed, what special precautions should be followed during the shutdown procedure?

When finished with the combustion heater, a cool-down period is required. Most heaters require that outside air be permitted to circulate through the unit for at least 15 seconds in flight, or that the ventilation fan be operated for at least 2 minutes on the ground.

Failure to provide an adequate cool-down will usually trip the thermal switch and render the heater inoperative until the switch is reset.

[PA.I.G, CA.I.G; FAA-H-8083-3]

7. How is a combustion heater prevented from operating in a potentially dangerous overheated condition?

Various automatic combustion heater controls prevent operation of the heater when dangerous conditions exist. As examples, the flow of fuel is cut off if there is insufficient combustion air, insufficient ventilating air, and in some cases if the ignition system is not operating. Other controls prevent too rapid heating of the combustion chamber and prevent exceeding a maximum output temperature. Normally, a thermal switch is mounted on the unit, which cannot be accessed in flight and requires the pilot or mechanic to actually visually inspect the unit for possible heat damage in order to reset the switch.

[PA.I.G, CA.I.G; FAA-H-8083-31]

8. Why is a preflight inspection of a nose baggage compartment important?

A thorough preflight of a nose baggage compartment is important to ensure that any baggage is secured and is within load limits, that latches are properly secured so that doors do not open during flight, and that any systems inside that area have been inspected. In many aircraft, heater systems and oxygen bottles are accessible through a nose baggage compartment. These may be critical items to include in a preflight and to ensure that any baggage in the area is properly secured so as to not do damage to these or affect their operation.

[PA.II.A, CA.II.A; FAA-H-8083-3]

J. Deicing and Anti-Icing

1. If an airplane has anti-icing and/or deicing equipment installed, can it be flown into icing conditions?

The presence of anti-icing and deicing equipment, even though it may appear elaborate and complete, does not necessarily mean that the airplane is approved for flight in icing conditions. The POH/AFM, placards, and even the manufacturer, should be consulted for specific determination of approvals and limitations. For an aircraft to be operated into known icing conditions, it will be certificated as capable of "flight into known icing (FIKI)."

[PA.I.G, CA.I.G; FAA-H-8083-3, POH/AFM]

2. Define the term *anti-icing*, and state several examples of the different types of anti-icing equipment found on multi-engine aircraft.

Anti-icing equipment is provided to prevent ice from forming on certain protected surfaces. Anti-icing equipment typically includes heated pitot tubes, heated or non-icing static ports and fuel vents, propeller blades with electro-thermal boots or alcohol slingers, windshields with alcohol spray or electrical resistance heating, windshield defoggers, and heated stall warning lift detectors.

[PA.I.G, CA.I.G; FAA-H-8083-3]

3. When should anti-icing equipment be activated?

In the absence of POH/AFM guidance to the contrary, anti-icing equipment is most effective when actuated prior to flight into suspected icing conditions. Anti-icing equipment is most commonly heated or liquid-deiced propeller or leading-edge surfaces, windshields, and/or pitot/static anti-icing and deicing equipment.

[PA.I.G, CA.I.G; FAA-H-8083-3]

4. Define the term *deicing*, and state several examples of the different types of deicing equipment found on multi-engine aircraft.

Deicing equipment is installed to remove ice that has already formed on protected surfaces. Surface deicing equipment most commonly covers wing leading edges and vertical and horizontal deicing of leading edges on the tail of the aircraft. This deicing is commonly accomplished by inflating boot systems or with liquid, alcohol-based fluid disbursement. In a few instances, the deicing may be accomplished by utilization of heated surfaces.

[PA.I.G, CA.I.G; FAA-H-8083-3]

5. Describe how deicing equipment works.

Upon pilot actuation, the boots inflate with air from the pneumatic pumps to break off accumulated ice. After a few seconds of inflation, they are deflated back to their normal position with the assistance of a vacuum. The pilot monitors the buildup of ice and cycles the boots as directed in the POH/AFM. These are not anti-icing tools but are intended to remove ice once it has built up.

[PA.I.G, CA.I.G; FAA-H-8083-3]

6. What are some examples of other types of equipment required for flight in icing conditions?

Other examples are an alternate induction air source, an alternate static system source, and ice tolerant antennas.

[PA.I.G, CA.I.G; FAA-H-8083-3]

7. What is the first indication that ice is accumulating over the normal engine air induction source?

Ice buildup on normal induction sources can be detected by a loss of engine RPM with fixed-pitch propellers and a loss of manifold pressure with constant-speed propellers. Carburetor heat (in carbureted engines) or alternate air (in fuel-injected engines) should be selected. On some fuel-injected engines, an alternate air source is automatically activated with blockage of the normal air source.

[PA.I.G, CA.I.G; FAA-H-8083-3]

8. Does the static system have any protection from icing?

The areas around the static ports may be heated with electric heater elements to prevent ice from forming over the port and blocking the entry of the static air. This is not present on all aircraft, especially in aircraft where the static port is positioned in such a way that it is less likely to accumulate icing.

[PA.I.G, CA.I.G; FAA-H-8083-15]

9. What is the recommended procedure for use of the autopilot in possible icing conditions?

Unless otherwise recommended in the POH/AFM, the autopilot should not be used in icing conditions. Continuous use of the autopilot will mask trim and handling changes that will occur with ice accumulation. Without this control feedback, the pilot might be unaware that ice accumulation is building to hazardous levels.

Exam Tip: Be prepared to answer questions about any and all equipment installed in the aircraft. For example, if your aircraft has an autopilot, have in-depth knowledge of its operation, even if you rarely use it. Also, if you don't know the answer to a system question, know how to find it. Have a POH or AFM readily available.

[PA.I.G, CA.I.G; FAA-H-8083-3]

K. Oxygen

1. What do the regulations require concerning flight crew's and passenger's oxygen use?

Regulations require, at a minimum, that flight crews have and use supplemental oxygen after 30 minutes exposure to cabin pressure altitudes between 12,500 and 14,000 feet. Use of supplemental oxygen is required immediately upon exposure to cabin pressure altitudes above 14,000 feet. Above 15,000 feet cabin pressure altitude, every aircraft occupant must have supplemental oxygen.

[PA.I.G, CA.I.G, PA.I.H, CA.I.H, PA.I.F, CA.I.H; FAA-H-8083-25]

2. What are the three basic components of an aircraft oxygen system?

Most oxygen systems (portable or installed) consist of three components:

a. A storage system (containers)
b. A delivery system
c. Mask or nasal cannula

[PA.I.G, CA.I.G, PA.I.H, CA.I.H, PA.I.F, CA.I.H; FAA-H-8083-25]

3. What are several types of oxygen systems in use?

Systems are often characterized by the type of regulator used to
dispense the oxygen:

a. Diluter-demand
b. Pressure-demand
c. Continuous-flow
d. Electrical pulse-demand

[PA.I.G, CA.I.G; FAA-H-8083-25, FAA-H-8083-31]

4. What are the components of a portable oxygen equipment system?

The portable equipment usually consists of a container, regulator,
mask outlet, and pressure gauge. Aircraft oxygen is usually stored
in high pressure system containers of 1,800 to 2,200 psi.

[PA.I.G, CA.I.G; FAA-H-8083-25]

5. Describe the diluter-demand oxygen system.

A diluter-demand oxygen system delivers oxygen mixed or diluted
with air in order to maintain a constant oxygen partial pressure as
the altitude changes. The demand mask provides a tight seal over
the face to prevent dilution with outside air and can be used safely
up to 40,000 feet.

[PA.I.G, CA.I.G; FAA-H-8083-25]

6. How does a pressure-demand oxygen system operate?

Pressure-demand oxygen systems are similar to diluter-demand
oxygen equipment, except that oxygen is supplied to the mask
under pressure at cabin altitudes above 34,000 feet. Pressure
demand regulators create airtight and oxygen-tight seals, but they
also provide a positive pressure application of oxygen to the mask
face piece that allows the user's lungs to be pressurized with
oxygen, making these systems safe at altitudes above 40,000 feet.

[PA.I.G, CA.I.G; FAA-H-8083-25, FAA-H-8083-31]

7. How do continuous-flow oxygen systems function?

A continuous-flow oxygen system supplies a constant supply of
pure oxygen to a rebreather bag that dilutes the pure oxygen with
exhaled gases and thus supplies a healthy mix of oxygen and
ambient air to the mask. It is primarily used in passenger cabins of
commercial airliners.

[PA.I.G, CA.I.G; FAA-H-8083-25]

8. Describe an electrical pulse-demand oxygen system.

Portable electrical pulse-demand oxygen systems deliver oxygen
by detecting an individual's inhalation effort and provide oxygen
flow during the initial portion of inhalation. Pulse demand systems
do not waste oxygen during the breathing cycle because oxygen
is only delivered during inhalation. Most pulse-demand oxygen
systems incorporate an internal barometer that automatically
compensates for changes in altitude by increasing the amount of
oxygen delivered for each pulse as altitude is increased.

[PA.I.G, CA.I.G; FAA-H-8083-25]

9. What are the various types of oxygen storage systems?

a. Gaseous aviator's breathing oxygen (ABO)
b. Liquid aviator's breathing oxygen (LOX)
c. Sodium chlorate candles (solid-state oxygen)
d. Molecular sieve oxygen generators (MSOG)

[PA.I.G, CA.I.G; FAA-H-8083-25]

10. Describe the PRICE acronym in relation to checking the aircraft oxygen system.

Pressure—Ensure that there is enough oxygen pressure and
quantity to complete the flight.

Regulator—Inspect the oxygen regulator for proper function. If
you are using a continuous-flow system, make sure the outlet
assembly and plug-in coupling are compatible.

Indicator—Most oxygen delivery systems indicate oxygen flow
by use of flow indicators. Flow indicators may be located on the
regulator or within the oxygen delivery tube. Don the mask and
check the flow indicator to assure a steady flow of oxygen.

Connections—Ensure that all connections are secured. This includes oxygen lines, plug-in coupling, and the mask.

Emergency—Have oxygen equipment in the aircraft ready to use for those emergencies that call for oxygen (hypoxia, decompression sickness, smoke and fumes, and rapid decompressions). This step should include briefing passengers on the location of oxygen and its proper use.

[PA.I.G, CA.I.G; FAA-H-8083-25]

L. Pressurization Systems

1. If a pilot is flying a pressurized aircraft, what parts of the aircraft are typically pressurized?

In a typical pressurization system, the cabin, flight compartment, and baggage compartments are incorporated into a sealed unit capable of containing air under a pressure higher than outside atmospheric pressure.

[PA.I.G, CA.I.G; FAA-H-8083-25]

2. How is pressurization of a cabin accomplished in a pressurized aircraft?

On aircraft powered by turbine engines, bleed air from the engine compressor section is used to pressurize the cabin. Superchargers may be used on older-model turbine-powered aircraft to pump air into the sealed fuselage. Piston-powered aircraft may use air supplied from each engine turbocharger through a sonic venturi (flow limiter).

[PA.I.G, CA.I.G; FAA-H-8083-25]

3. What is a typical altitude a cabin pressurization system should be able to maintain at operating or maximum designed cruising speed for an aircraft?

A cabin pressurization system typically maintains a cabin pressure altitude of approximately 8,000 feet at the maximum designed cruising altitude of an aircraft. This prevents rapid changes of cabin altitude that may be uncomfortable or cause injury to passengers and crew. In addition, the pressurization system permits a reasonably fast exchange of air from the inside to the outside of the cabin. If the aircraft is not maintaining this or a lower cabin pressure altitude at this or lower altitudes, it is likely an indication that there is a leak in the system or that the system is not generating enough pressure.

[PA.I.G, CA.I.G; FAA-H-8083-25]

4. What is meant by the term *cabin pressure* when referring to operations in a pressurized aircraft?

This is the cabin pressure in terms of equivalent altitude above sea level as experienced in the cabin due to the operation of the pressurization system.

[PA.I.G, CA.I.G; FAA-H-8083-25]

5. What is meant by the term *differential pressure* when referring to operations in a pressurized aircraft?

This is the difference in pressure between the pressure acting on one side of a wall and the pressure acting on the other side of the wall. In aircraft air-conditioning and pressurizing systems, it is the difference between cabin pressure and atmospheric pressure.

[PA.I.G, CA.I.G; FAA-H-8083-25]

6. What is the main danger that a pilot would experience with the failure of a pressurization system while operating at higher altitudes?

The primary danger of decompression is hypoxia. Quick, proper utilization of oxygen equipment is necessary to avoid unconsciousness. Another potential danger that pilots, crew, and passengers face during high-altitude decompressions is evolved gas decompression sickness.

[PA.I.G, CA.I.G; FAA-H-8083-25]

7. A pilot who encounters rapid or even slow decompression may need to execute what maneuver?

To allow the pilot to get safely to an appropriate altitude where hypoxia is no longer a risk, an emergency descent may be necessary if operating in an area where terrain allows it. During this activity, the pilot may also make use of supplemental oxygen as directed by the manufacturer's AFM/POH or available equipment.

[PA.I.G, CA.I.G, PA.IX.A, CA.IX.A; FAA-H-8083-25, AFM/POH]

Multi-Engine Aerodynamics and Inoperative Engine Procedures

3

A. Multi-Engine Aerodynamic Factors

1. What are the effects of P-factor in a multi-engine airplane equipped with non-counter-rotating propellers?

The descending propeller blade of each engine will produce greater thrust than the ascending blade when the airplane is operated under power and at positive angles of attack. The descending propeller blade of the right engine is also a greater distance from the center of gravity and therefore has a longer moment arm than the descending propeller blade of the left engine. As a result, failure of the left engine will result in the most asymmetrical thrust (adverse yaw), as the right engine will be providing the remaining thrust.

[PA.X.B, CA.X.B; FAA-H-8083-3]

2. What does it mean when an engine is described as a *critical engine*?

In the context of multi-engine aircraft, the term *critical engine* refers to the engine that, if it were to fail, would have the most adverse effect on the performance and controllability of the aircraft, especially during takeoff, climb-out, or high angle of attack operations.

The critical engine is typically determined by factors such as the aircraft's design, the engine placement, and the direction of propeller rotation. For example, in a twin-engine aircraft with engines mounted on the wings, the critical engine is often the engine that, if it fails, creates more yawing or rolling moment.

Typically, in most conventional twin-engine aircraft, these factors will make the left engine the critical engine.

[PA.X.B, CA.X.B; FAA-H-8083-3]

3. What four aerodynamic factors make an engine a critical engine?

When referring to the critical engine, four aerodynamic factors are typically considered. Many multi-engine pilots use the mnemonic "PAST" to help them remember these factors: **P**-factor, **A**ccelerated slipstream, **S**piraling slipstream, and **T**orque effect.

P-factor (yawing moment) — P-factor is an aerodynamic effect caused by the asymmetric thrust produced by a propeller. At low airspeeds and high angles of attack, the effective thrust centerline shifts to the right on each engine because the descending propeller blades produce more thrust than the ascending blades (P-factor). The right-shifting thrust of the right engine operates at a greater moment arm than the left engine, which creates a greater yawing force if the left engine fails.

Accelerated slipstream (rolling moment)—As a result of P-factor, stronger induced lift is produced on the descending blade by its prop wash. When both engines are operating normally, the slipstream generated by each engine's propeller flows around the aircraft symmetrically. However, in the event of an engine failure or asymmetric thrust condition (such as during takeoff or a single-engine operation), the slipstream from the operating engine(s) becomes more pronounced on one side of the aircraft. P-factor thrust causes more thrust on the side of the descending blade. As a result, the right wing's center of lift will be further from the longitudinal axis and the left wing's center of lift will be closer. Failure of the left engine will produce more of a rolling moment than failure of the right engine.

Spiraling slipstream (yawing moment)—The spiraling slipstream is the rotational airflow generated by the spinning propeller. This airflow pattern can affect the aerodynamics of the aircraft, particularly at low airspeeds and high angles of attack. The spiraling slipstream from the left engine strikes the vertical stabilizer from the left, yawing the aircraft to the left and counteracting the yaw produced in a right engine failure. In a left engine failure, the spiraling slipstream from the right engine hits nothing and drifts away. It does not help counteract the yaw toward the dead engine.

Torque effect (rolling moment)—The clockwise-turning propeller produces counterclockwise rolling. Losing the left engine means yaw and roll to the left. Torque effect is another asymmetric force generated by the engine and propeller system. In a single-engine aircraft, torque effect typically causes the aircraft to yaw to the left due to the engine and propeller rotation. In multi-engine aircraft with counter-rotating propellers, torque effect can still influence aircraft behavior, but it is less pronounced. However, during engine-out scenarios, torque effect can become significant, especially if one engine fails.

(continued)

The placement of engines on the aircraft's wings or fuselage can also influence which engine is critical. Factors such as the distance between engines, wing design, and aircraft symmetry play a role. Engines mounted farther from the aircraft's centerline may have a greater effect on aircraft stability and control during engine-out situations.

[PA.X.B, CA.X.B; FAA-H-8083-3]

4. What does V_{MC} mean for a multi-engine pilot?

V_{MC} stands for "minimum control speed with critical engine inoperative." It is a critical concept for pilots of multi-engine aircraft, particularly during single-engine operations or engine-out scenarios.

V_{MC} represents the minimum airspeed at which the pilot can maintain control of the aircraft with the critical engine (the engine that, if it fails, would have the most adverse effect on aircraft control and performance) inoperative and the remaining engine(s) at full power. Below V_{MC}, the asymmetric thrust and aerodynamic forces generated by the operating engine(s) become too great for the pilot to counteract with rudder input alone, leading to a loss of directional control.

Several factors affect V_{MC}, including aircraft weight, configuration (such as flap settings and landing gear position), density altitude, and center of gravity location. Pilots must be aware of these factors and ensure that the aircraft remains above V_{MC} during critical phases of flight, such as takeoff, initial climb, and any other situation where an engine failure could occur.

It's important to note that V_{MC} is not a fixed value but rather a speed range. The aircraft's pilot's operating handbook (POH) or airplane flight manual (AFM) provides specific V_{MC} values for various configurations and conditions. Pilots undergo training to recognize and respond to V_{MC}-related situations, including techniques for maintaining control and performing emergency procedures in the event of an engine failure.

Flight test pilots' determination of V_{MC} in airplane certification is solely concerned with the minimum speed for directional control under one very specific set of circumstances. V_{MC} has nothing to do with climb performance, nor is it the optimum airplane attitude, bank angle, ball position, or configuration for best climb performance.

[PA.X.B, CA.X.B; FAA-H-8083-3]

5. How is V_{MC} determined by the manufacturer for a multi-engine aircraft?

The method used to simulate critical engine failure must represent the most critical mode of powerplant failure expected in service with respect to controllability. V_{MC} for takeoff must not exceed 1.2 V_{S1}, where V_{S1} is determined at the maximum takeoff weight. V_{MC} must be determined with the:

a. Most unfavorable weight;

b. Most unfavorable center of gravity position;

c. Airplane airborne and ground effect negligible;

d. Maximum available takeoff power initially on each engine;

e. Airplane trimmed for takeoff;

f. Flaps in the takeoff position;

g. Landing gear retracted; and

h. All propeller controls in the recommended takeoff position throughout.

At V_{MC}, the rudder pedal force required to maintain control must not exceed 150 pounds, and it must not be necessary to reduce power of the operative engine(s). During the maneuver, the airplane must not assume any dangerous attitude and it must be possible to prevent a heading change of more than 20 degrees.

Note: V_{MC} only addresses directional control. There is no requirement in the determination of V_{MC} that the airplane be capable of climbing.

[PA.X.B, CA.X.B; 14 CFR 23.149, 25.149, FAA-H-8083-3]

6. What factors affect V_{MC}?

a. Power
b. Propeller (windmilling or feathered)
c. Weight
d. Center-of-gravity position
e. Density altitude
f. Sideslip condition
g. Flap position
h. Landing gear position

[PA.X.B, CA.X.B; FAA-H-8083-3]

7. What are the aerodynamic effects of changes in configuration of the aircraft on V_{MC} speed?

Exam tip: Be prepared to describe how changing configuration of flaps, gear, propeller settings, and aircraft loading may affect what a real effective V_{MC} speed might be compared with the published V_{MC} from the manufacturer.

Generally, conditions that lower V_{MC} *increase* control, but *decrease* performance. For example, a forward CG will increase rudder effectiveness due to a longer arm. Higher density altitude will decrease engine power and thrust. Reduction of power on an operating engine will decrease asymmetric thrust, and feathering the engine on the failed engine will reduce drag and yaw. Being at a higher or even maximum takeoff weight will help resist yaw. Deploying flaps will increase lift but also increase drag. Putting a gear down when possible will increase drag but will also help resist roll motion for the aircraft. Each of these effects positively or negatively affect the performance and controllability of the aircraft.

Typically, a V_{MC} as published will be higher than one that would be experienced when flying on a single engine in flight or for an approach after a pilot has feathered the inoperative engine, reduced power on the operating engine, put the gear down, and/or put the manufacturer's recommend flap setting down for a landing. While not as common, in a larger aircraft a pilot could choose to shift weight and balance distribution forward to further assist aerodynamic stability.

[PA.X.B, CA.X.B; FAA-H-8083-3]

8. **During an engine-out emergency, what configuration factors produce the most drag and what might be the effect on climb (or generated descent) performance?**

Sample items from one popular light twin POH and their effects in the form of increased descent values due to drag:

Windmilling propeller	400 fpm
Landing gear extended	300 fpm
Extended flaps	150 to 550 fpm
Flight control positions (to counteract yawing and rolling tendencies)	as much as 300 fpm

Note: The above performance values will vary for different aircraft. For accuracy, you should review your particular AFM. Examiners ask this question to confirm that applicants know what the high and low drag items are on the airplane. An actual inflight demonstration is always the most accurate method of determining actual performance loss values for a given aircraft in an engine-out situation.

[PA.X.B, CA.X.B; FAA-H-8083-3]

9. **What would cause V_{MC} to be higher than stated in the POH/AFM?**

a. *Maximum available takeoff power*—V_{MC} increases as power is increased on the operating engine.

b. *Critical engine propeller windmilling*—V_{MC} increases with increased drag on the inoperative engine.

c. *Most unfavorable weight*—V_{MC} increases as weight is reduced.

d. *Center-of-gravity position*—V_{MC} increases as the center of gravity is moved aft.

e. *Density altitude*—V_{MC} increases with a decrease in density altitude (increase in air density).

f. *Sideslip condition*—V_{MC} increases significantly with decreases in bank angle.

Note: Any possible benefit that extended flaps and/or extended gear may have on V_{MC} and directional control is greatly offset by the decrease in climb performance as a result of the increased drag.

(continued)

The effect of flaps and/or gear extended versus retracted on V_{MC} is not determined in the certification process.

[PA.X.B, CA.X.B; FAA-H-8083-3]

10. Explain why the movement of the center of gravity (CG) affects V_{MC}.

V_{MC} increases as the CG is moved aft. The moment arm of the rudder is reduced, and therefore its effectiveness is reduced, as the CG is moved aft. For a typical light twin, the aft-most CG limit is the most unfavorable CG position.

[PA.X.B, CA.X.B; FAA-H-8083-3]

11. Why does a change in weight affect V_{MC}?

V_{MC} is unaffected by weight in straight-and-level flight. V_{MC} will be affected by the aircraft's weight in turning (banked) flight. When an aircraft is banked, a component of the aircraft weight acts with the horizontal component of lift to create a more effective sideslip toward the operative engine. V_{MC} increases as weight is reduced. Currently, 14 CFR Part 23 calls for V_{MC} to be determined at the most unfavorable weight. For twins certificated under CAR 3 or early 14 CFR Part 23, the weight at which V_{MC} was determined was not specified.

[PA.X.B, CA.X.B; FAA-H-8083-3]

12. Why does a change in density altitude affect V_{MC}?

For an airplane with non-turbocharged engines, V_{MC} decreases as density altitude increases. Consequently, directional control can be maintained at a lower airspeed than at sea level. This is because since power decreases with altitude, the thrust moment of the operating engine lessens, thereby reducing the need for the yawing force of the rudder.

[PA.X.B, CA.X.B; FAA-H-8083-3]

13. How does a windmilling propeller affect V_{MC}?

A windmilling propeller will generate significant drag, resulting in less directional control and a higher V_{MC}.

[PA.X.B, CA.X.B; FAA-H-8083-3]

14. How does a sideslip condition affect V_{MC}?

Engine inoperative flight with wings level and ball centered requires large rudder input toward the operative engine. The result is a moderate sideslip toward the inoperative engine. Climb performance will be reduced by the moderate sideslip. With wings level, V_{MC} will be significantly higher than published as there is no horizontal component of lift available to help the rudder combat asymmetrical thrust.

[PA.X.B, CA.X.B; FAA-H-8083-3]

15. Explain the relationship between your aircraft's published V_{MC} speed and its stall speed (V_S) as altitude increases.

With normally aspirated engines, V_{MC} decreases with altitude. Stalling speed (V_S), however, remains the same. Except for a few models, published V_{MC} is almost always higher than V_S. At sea level, there is usually a margin of several knots between V_{MC} and V_S, but the margin decreases with altitude, and at some altitude, V_{MC} and V_S are the same.

[PA.X.B, CA.X.B; FAA-H-8083-3]

16. During a training flight, what conditions would make a V_{MC} demonstration inadvisable?

Since V_{MC} is a function of power (which decreases with altitude), it is possible for the airplane to reach a stall speed prior to loss of directional control. It must be understood that there is a certain density altitude above which the stalling speed is higher than the engine-out minimum control speed. During a typical V_{MC} demonstration, with one engine feathered and the aircraft slowing to V_{MC}, a stall would occur first, followed by a very strong tendency for the aircraft to roll. This situation would almost certainly guarantee a spin condition which could be difficult to correct. When this density altitude (due to high elevations or temperatures) exists close to the ground or at altitude, an effective flight demonstration of loss of directional control may be hazardous and should not be attempted.

[PA.X.B, CA.X.B; FAA-H-8083-3]

17. During a V_{MC} demonstration with the left propeller feathered, you encounter stall indications before reaching V_{MC}. Describe what will happen next.

A pilot conducting a V_{MC} demonstration with the left engine propeller feathered is simulating the failure of the critical engine of the aircraft. When doing so, if the pilot is encountering indications of a stall, it is an indication that they are approaching exceedance of the critical angle of attack for the aircraft in that configuration. When this happens, the pilot should respond by reducing the angle of attack and potentially simultaneously reducing the throttle on the "good" engine—in this case, the right engine. This reduces the rolling motion caused by the right engine that is still generating power. Once the aircraft has regained level flight and is at a lower angle of attack, power may be reintroduced on the good engine at an angle of attack that does not generate a stalling condition.

[PA.X.B, CA.X.B; FAA-P-8740-66]

18. Discuss the advantages/disadvantages of operating at less than gross weight with one engine inoperative.

Operating a multi-engine aircraft with one engine inoperative significantly decreases the performance of the aircraft due to lack of available horsepower. Any reduction in weight of the aircraft will allow for great climb ability, but it also affects the realized V_{MC} characteristics of the aircraft. A lower weight allows an aircraft to be more easily dislodged from stable flight and thus under single-engine operations actually increase the potential to experience a V_{MC} condition.

[PA.I.F, CA.I.F, PA.X.B, CA.X.B, PA.IX.F, CA.IX.F; FAAH-8083-3]

19. What technique should be used when making a turn with one engine inoperative?

When making turns under single-engine operating conditions, it is suggested that pilots keep bank angles to a minimum due to an increased risk of a V_{MC} condition at higher bank angles. Turns should be made in trim and avoiding sideslip conditions during the maneuvers. A turn into the "good" engine will typically be less likely to induce a V_{MC} condition, while a turn into the "bad" (or dead) engine may increase the potential for encountering a V_{MC} condition.

[PA.I.A, CA.I.A; FAA-H-8083-3]

20. What are the operational advantages of an aircraft equipped with counter-rotating propellers?

The main advantage of an aircraft equipped with counter-rotating propellers is the distinct advantage of not having a critical engine because of the balancing of both torque and P-factor. The thrust line of either engine is the same distance from the centerline of the fuselage, so there will be no difference in yaw effect between loss of the left or the right engine.

[PA.X.B, CA.X.B; FAA-H-8083-3]

21. Discuss the use of power during approach and landing in a multi-engine airplane.

The final approach should be made with power and at a speed recommended by the manufacturer; if a recommended speed is not furnished, the speed should be no slower than the single-engine best rate-of-climb speed (V_{YSE}) until short final with the landing assured, but in no case less than critical engine-out minimum control speed (V_{MC}).

In the round-out for landing, residual power should be gradually reduced to idle. With the higher wing loading and the drag from two windmilling propellers, there will be minimal float. Full stall landings are generally undesirable in twins.

[PA.IX.G, CA.IX.G; FAA-H-8083-3]

22. How is the best single-engine climb performance obtained?

Best single-engine climb performance is obtained at V_{YSE} with maximum available power and minimum drag. After the flaps and landing gear have been retracted and the propeller of the failed engine feathered, a key element in getting best climb performance is to minimize sideslip.

Note: V_{YSE} *theoretically* provides the greatest altitude gain when only one engine is operating, but it does not guarantee that you will be able to climb or even maintain altitude on one engine. Before taking the runway, you should know if the airplane could reasonably be expected to continue its climb following an engine failure.

[PA.IX.F, CA.IX.F; FAA-P-8740-66, FAA Safety ALC-30]

23. **With one engine inoperative, how can the pilot determine that the aircraft is in a minimum or zero sideslip condition?**

In a multi-engine airplane with an inoperative engine, the centered ball is no longer the indicator of zero sideslip due to asymmetrical thrust. In fact, no instrument will directly tell the pilot the flight conditions for zero sideslip. Without a yaw string, minimizing sideslip is a matter of placing the airplane at a predetermined bank angle and ball position.

[PA.IX.F, CA.IX.F; FAA-H-8083-3]

24. **What two control inputs will you use to achieve a zero sideslip condition?**

There are two different control inputs that can be used to counteract the asymmetrical thrust of a failed engine: yaw from the rudder, and the horizontal component of lift that results from bank with the ailerons. Used individually, neither is correct. Used together in the proper combination, zero sideslip and best climb performance are achieved.

[PA.IX.F, CA.IX.F; FAA-H-8083-3]

25. **What speed does the blue line on an airspeed indicator designate?**

Best single-engine rate-of-climb speed (V_{YSE}), which delivers the greatest gain in altitude in the shortest possible time with one engine inoperative. V_{YSE} also yields the minimum rate of sink with one engine inoperative.

[PA.IX.F, CA.IX.F; FAA-H-8083-3]

26. **What speed does the red line on an airspeed indicator designate?**

Minimum control speed with the critical engine inoperative (V_{MC}) indicates the minimum control speed, airborne at sea level with the critical engine inoperative.

[PA.X.B, CA.X.B; FAA-P-8740-66, FAA-H-8083-3]

B. Inoperative Engine Directional Control

1. What three performance/control problems must a pilot deal with immediately after the loss of one engine on a multi-engine aircraft?

The loss of power on one engine affects both climb performance and controllability of any light twin. The following problems will occur:

a. Loss of climb performance (at least 80 percent).

b. A yawing moment toward the inoperative engine (due to asymmetric thrust).

c. A rolling moment toward the inoperative engine (due to loss of induced airflow).

[PA.IX.F, CA.IX.F; FAA-P-8740-66]

2. Describe the indications a pilot would notice as a multi-engine airplane, with one-engine inoperative, approaches V_{MC}.

a. Increased yawing tendency.

b. Rapid decay in control effectiveness.

c. Symptoms of an impending stall—stall warning light/horn, airframe or elevator buffet.

d. Full rudder travel has been reached and airplane is still yawing toward inoperative engine.

[PA.IX.F, CA.IX.F; FAA-H-8083-3]

3. Why does a multi-engine airplane, with one engine inoperative, become directionally uncontrollable during flight at an airspeed less than V_{MC}?

When one engine fails, the pilot must overcome the asymmetrical thrust (except on airplanes with centerline thrust) created by the operating engine by setting up a counteracting moment with the rudder. When the rudder is fully deflected, its yawing power will depend upon the velocity of airflow across the rudder, which in turn is dependent upon the airspeed. As the airplane decelerates, it will reach a speed below which the rudder moment will no longer balance the thrust moment, and directional control will be lost.

[PA.X.B, CA.X.B; FAA-H-8083-3]

4. **Why does a multi-engine airplane with one engine inoperative roll in the direction of the inoperative engine?**

Loss of power on one engine reduces the induced airflow from the propeller slipstream over that wing. As a result, total lift for that wing is substantially reduced, causing the airplane to roll in the direction of the inoperative engine. Yaw also affects the lift distribution over the wing, causing a roll toward the dead engine. These roll forces may be balanced by banking into the operative engine as well as application of rudder opposite to the direction of yaw.

[PA.X.B, CA.X.B; FAA-P-8740-66]

5. **What causes a spin to occur?**

A spin occurs when the airplane's wing exceeds its critical angle of attack (stall) with a sideslip or yaw acting on the airplane at or beyond the actual stall. During this uncoordinated maneuver, a pilot may not be aware that a critical angle of attack has been exceeded until the airplane yaws out of control toward the lowering wing. If stall recovery is not initiated immediately, the airplane may enter a spin. In a multi-engine airplane, the yawing moment may be generated by rudder input or asymmetrical thrust.

[PA.VII.D, CA.VII.E; FAA-H-8083-3]

6. **Describe several flight situations where unintentional spins may occur.**

Spin awareness must be at its greatest during V_{MC} demonstrations, stall practice, slow flight, or any condition of high asymmetrical thrust, particularly at low speed/high angle of attack. Single-engine stalls are not part of any multi-engine training curriculum.

[PA.VII.D, CA.VII.E; FAA-H-8083-3]

7. **What multi-engine flight training procedure may inadvertently degrade into a spin?**

A simulated engine failure introduced at an inappropriately low speed. No engine failure should ever be introduced below safe, intentional one engine inoperative speed (V_{SSE}). If no V_{SSE} is published, use V_{YSE}.

[PA.VII.D, CA.VII.E; FAA-H-8083-3]

8. **Describe the entry, incipient, and developed phases of a spin.**

Entry phase—The pilot intentionally or accidentally provides the necessary elements (exceeding critical angle of attack, full stall, applying excessive or insufficient rudder/aileron) for the spin.

Incipient spin—That portion of a spin from the time the airplane stalls and rotation starts until the spin becomes fully developed.

Fully developed, steady-state spin—Occurs when the aircraft angular rotation rate, airspeed, and vertical speed are stabilized from turn-to-turn in a flight path that is close to vertical.

[PA.VII.D, CA.VII.E; AC 61-67, FAA-H-8083-3]

9. **What procedure is recommended for recovering from an inadvertent spin?**

If a spin is entered, most manufacturers recommend immediately retarding both throttles to idle, applying full rudder opposite the direction of rotation, and applying full forward elevator/stabilator pressure (with ailerons neutral). These actions should be taken as near simultaneously as possible, and the controls should then be held in that position until the spin has stopped. At that point, the pilot should adjust rudder pressure, back elevator pressure, and power as necessary to return to the desired flight path. Spin recovery will take considerable altitude; therefore, it is critical that corrective action be taken immediately.

Note: No multi-engine airplane is approved for spins, and their spin recovery characteristics are generally very poor. It is therefore necessary to practice spin avoidance and maintain a high awareness of situations that can result in an inadvertent spin.

[PA.VII.D, CA.VII.E; FAA-H-8083-3]

10. **After an engine failure has occurred, explain why it's necessary to feather the failed engine's propeller as soon as possible.**

    At the smaller blade angles near the flat pitch position, the drag added by an unfeathered propeller is very large. At these small blade angles, the propeller windmilling at high RPM can create such a tremendous amount of drag that the airplane may be uncontrollable. The propeller windmilling at high speed in the low range of blade angles can produce an increase in parasite drag that may be as great as the parasite drag of the basic airplane.

    [PA.IX.F, CA.IX.F; FAA-H-8083-3]

11. **Why is it necessary to bank toward the operative engine in an engine-out emergency?**

    If the wings are kept level and the ball in the turn coordinator centered, the airplane will be in a moderate sideslip toward the inoperative engine, resulting in a substantial increase in V_{MC} and a significant reduction in climb and/or acceleration capability. By establishing a bank toward the operative engine, a component of the aircraft's weight is utilized to counteract the rudder-induced sideforce present in the sideslip. At a specific angle of bank, the airplane will be in a zero-sideslip condition, leading to adequate directional control as well as a substantial increase in engine-out performance (rate of climb). Decreasing the bank angle away from the operative engine increases V_{MC} at the rate of approximately 3 knots per degree of bank.

    Note: Banking into the operative engine, beyond that necessary for a zero-sideslip condition, may increase rudder authority and assist in directional control initially but it will also *drastically* reduce the airplane's climb performance. Once directional control has been achieved, a reduction in bank angle, as necessary to achieve a zero-sideslip condition, must be established in order to obtain the necessary climb performance.

    [PA.X.B, CA.X.B; FAA-H-8083-3, FAA-P-8740-66]

12. **In an engine-out emergency, what is the correct amount of bank angle and ball displacement to establish a zero-sideslip condition?**

    The precise condition of zero sideslip (bank angle and ball position) varies slightly from model to model and with available power and airspeed. If the airplane is not equipped with counter-rotating propellers, it will also vary slightly with the engine failed due to P-factor. The actual bank angle for zero sideslip varies among airplanes from one and one-half to two and one-half degrees. The position of the ball varies from one-third to one-half of a ball width from instrument center.

[PA.X.B, CA.X.B; FAA-H-8083-3]

13. How much of an increase in V_{MC} will occur if a bank toward the operative engine is not established?

Flight tests have shown that holding the ball of the turn coordinator in the center while maintaining heading with the wings level drastically increases V_{MC} as much as 20 knots in some airplanes.

[PA.X.B, CA.X.B; FAA-H-8083-3]

C. Engine-Out Operations

1. State three major causes of fatalities in engine-out emergencies.

Fatalities usually occur due to any one or combination of the following:

a. Loss of directional control.
b. Loss of climb performance.
c. Loss of flying airspeed.

[PA.X.B, CA.X.B, PA.IX.F, CA.IX.F; FAA-H-8083-3]

2. At what point, in terms of airspeed, is an engine failure on takeoff considered to be most critical?

The most critical time for a one engine inoperative condition in a multi-engine airplane is during the two- or three-second period immediately following liftoff while the airplane is accelerating to climb-out speed. Although most multi-engine airplanes are controllable at a speed close to the single-engine minimum control speed, the performance is often so far below optimum that continued flight following takeoff might be marginal or impossible.

[PA.X.B, CA.X.B; FAA-P-8740-66]

3. Describe how you can mitigate risks associated with an engine failure during or immediately after takeoff.

a. Always conduct a thorough pre-takeoff briefing (or self-briefing) prior to take-off. The briefing should include the PIC's plan of action in the event an actual engine failure or other emergency occurs during any phase of the takeoff and initial climb.

b. If a second pilot is available, discuss pilot flying and pilot not flying duties in the event of an emergency.

c. Know the performance capabilities for your airplane under the proposed flight conditions if an engine should fail at any time during the takeoff or initial climb. This should include accelerate-stop and accelerate-go distances, single-engine service ceiling, expected OEI rate of climb, and terrain or obstacles in the flight path. Factor in significant margins to adjust for real-world performance.

d. Prior to takeoff, know what your available options are in the event of an engine failure (runway length, direction of flight that is free of obstacles, etc.).

e. Maintain proficiency in engine-out emergency procedures for your aircraft.

[PA.IX.F, CA.IX.F; FAA-P-8740-66]

4. Are most light multi-engine aircraft required to demonstrate a single-engine climb?

No. Many pilots erroneously believe that because a light twin has two engines, it will continue to perform at least half as well with only one of those engines operating. There is nothing in 14 CFR Part 23, governing the certification of light twins, that requires an airplane to maintain altitude while in the takeoff configuration and with one engine inoperative. In fact, many current light twins are not required to do this with one engine inoperative in any configuration, even at sea level. This is of major significance in the operations of light twins certificated under Part 23. With regard to performance (but not controllability) in the takeoff or landing configuration, the light twin-engine airplane is, in concept, merely a single-engine airplane with its power divided into two units.

[PA.IX.F, CA.IX.F; FAA-H-8083-3]

5. What items on the single-engine emergency checklist should be committed to memory?

The memory items from the "engine failure after takeoff" checklist should be promptly executed to configure the airplane for climb. The specific procedures to follow will be found in the POH/AFM and checklist for the particular airplane.

A typical "engine failure" emergency checklist is depicted below. **Bold-faced** items require immediate action and are to be accomplished from memory.

Control	Maintain/return aircraft to level flight.
Performance	Maintain V_{YSE} or greater speed.
Mixture	Set mixtures full rich.
Propellers	Set propellers high RPM.
Throttles	Set throttles full power.
Gear Position	Gear retracted (Up)
Flaps Position	Flaps retracted (Up)
Identify	Determine which engine has lost power.
Verify	Verify which engine has lost power using throttle.
Fix or Feather	Choose (if at higher altitude) if there is time to attempt to fix the condition, or (if at low altitude) if immediate feathering of the affected engine is required.
Checklist	At higher altitude, complete an engine failure diagnosis checklist or securing checklist if unsuccessful at remedy or restart. At lower altitude, as time allows, complete any securing checklist.

This checklist should be a memorized process that gets the pilot to the "Fix or Feather" step, at which they would make a decision about how to proceed. The steps ahead of this one are memory items intended to have the pilot put the aircraft into the most favorable performance condition that is least likely to result in loss of controllability of the aircraft as they manage an engine failure or loss of power condition.

[PA.IX.F, CA.IX.F; FAA-H-8083-3]

6. **During a V_{MC} demonstration, what procedure should be followed if indications of an impending stall occur?**

The moment a pilot first recognizes uncontrollable yaw or experiences any symptom associated with a stall, the pilot should retard the throttle for the operating engine to stop the yaw as the pitch attitude is decreased. Recovery is made to straight flight on the entry heading at V_{SSE} or V_{YSE}, before setting symmetrical power. The recovery demonstration does not include increasing power on the windmilling engine alone.

Exam Tip: During the oral exam, be prepared to explain the inflight procedure you will use to demonstrate V_{MC}.

[PA.X.B, CA.X.B; FAA-H-8083-3]

7. **When an actual demonstration of V_{MC} is not possible due to certain conditions of density altitude, or in an airplane whose V_{MC} is equal to or less than V_S, what training technique can be used to enhance safety during the demonstration?**

A demonstration of V_{MC} may be safely conducted by artificially limiting rudder travel to simulate maximum available rudder. Limiting rudder travel should be accomplished at a speed well above V_S (approximately 20 knots). The rudder-limiting technique avoids the hazards of spinning as a result of stalling with high asymmetrical power, yet is effective in demonstrating the loss of directional control.

[PA.X.B, CA.X.B; FAA-H-8083-3]

8. **While performing a V_{MC} demonstration, the airplane begins to show signs of an impending stall, but you are focused on maintaining directional control and don't immediately notice the indications. Discuss what will happen next and what action you should take.**

If a pilot conducting a V_{MC} demonstration fails to notice or correct for a stall as it begins to occur, the left-turning tendencies associated with operating on a single engine will begin to overcome the pilot's ability to keep the aircraft from a rolling and yawing motion. This can lead to roll over, stall, and spin of the aircraft. To reduce the left-turning tendencies, the pilot should reduce power on the operative engine (typically both throttles to avoid any potential confusion), reduce the angle of attack, and establish an airspeed greater than V_{MC}, preferably at or above V_{YSE}, and stabilize the aircraft into level flight. Once this has been done, the pilot can choose to reintroduce power on the "good" engine while maintaining a proper angle of attack and airspeed.

[PA.X.B, CA.X.B; FAA-H-8083-3]

9. **What immediate actions must be taken if loss of one engine occurs below V_{MC}?**

If an engine fails below V_{MC} while the airplane is on the ground, the takeoff must be rejected. Directional control can only be maintained by promptly closing both throttles and using rudder and brakes as required. If an engine fails below V_{MC} while airborne, directional control is not possible with the remaining engine producing takeoff power. On takeoffs, therefore, the airplane should never be airborne before the airspeed reaches and exceeds V_{MC}.

[PA.X.B, CA.X.B; FAA-H-8083-3]

10. **Under what condition should stalls never be practiced in a multi-engine airplane?**

It is generally advised that pilots not practice stalling maneuvers under single-engine conditions, either actual or simulated, due to the danger of a V_{MC} condition and the significant altitude that might be required for recovery.

[PA.X.B, CA.X.B; FAA-H-8083-3]

11. **While performing steep turns, the inboard (lower) engine suddenly loses power. Explain what would happen next and the actions you would take to recover control of the aircraft.**

Due to the increased risk of a stall during a steep turn, a pilot who encounters any loss of power on an engine should immediately reduce the bank angle and return to level flight. The potential to encounter a V_{MC} if the engine fails during a steep turn is greater than during level flight. If the pilot encountered the engine failure on the "high wing" of the steep turn, the "low wing" that was still generating power would tend to bring the aircraft in a rolling motion back toward level flight. If, however, the low wing was the engine that encountered the power failure, the higher position and rolling position of the engine on the high wing during a steep turn could more easily generate additional rolling motion and exacerbate the condition into a V_{MC} encounter. If this occurs, the pilot might additionally choose to reduce power on the engine generating thrust (or both engines until level flight is established if altitude allows) to minimize this risk.

[PA.V.A, CA.V.A, PA.X.B, CA.X.B; FAA-H-8083-3, FAA-P-8740-66]

12. What is the pilot's first priority following an engine failure?

Maintain aircraft control and airspeed.

[PA.X.B, CA.X.B; FAA-H-8083-3]

13. Before feathering a suspected inoperative engine, what action should be taken first?

Verify which engine has failed by closing the throttle on the suspected dead engine.

[PA.X.A, CA.X.A; FAA-H-8083-3]

14. In the event of an engine failure, what methods may be used to positively identify the inoperative engine?

An inoperative engine can be identified by:

a. A definite yaw and roll toward the inoperative engine.

b. The old adage "dead foot, dead engine" may be used. The foot that is not applying rudder pressure indicates the side on which the engine has failed.

c. Verification; retard the throttle of the suspected engine before shutting it down. If no change in control input is necessary, this is the side on which an engine has failed.

[PA.X.A, CA.X.A; FAA-H-8083-3]

15. Why is use of the manifold pressure (MP) and RPM gauges problematic when attempting to identify an inoperative engine during an engine failure?

Depending on the failure mode (partial, complete), the pilot won't be able to consistently identify the failed engine in a timely manner by referencing the engine gauges. Depending on the type of failure (partial, complete), the manifold pressure gauge on an inoperative engine could initially indicate a pressure that could be similar to the MP indication on the operative engine. The propeller on the inoperative engine could be windmilling and indicating relatively high RPMs, leading the pilot to believe that the engine is still producing power.

[PA.X.A, CA.X.A; FAA-H-8083-3]

16. Which direction would the rudder be applied if the right engine failed?

The aircraft would yaw to the right, requiring application of left rudder pressure immediately.

[PA.X.A, CA.X.A; FAA-H-8083-3]

17. In the event of an engine failure in instrument meteorological conditions (IMC), what methods should be used to positively identify the inoperative engine?

Methods used for inoperative engine identification in visual meteorological conditions (V_{MC}) also apply to flight in IMC. Give priority to scanning your flight instruments, ensuring that heading and airspeed are maintained. Control the heading primarily with rudder pressure. The airplane will yaw in the direction of the failed engine. The turn coordinator ball will swing toward the operative engine due to centrifugal force. As always, rudder pressure will assist you in identifying the inoperative engine (dead foot, dead engine).

[PA.X.A, CA.X.A; FAA-H-8083-3]

18. When would V_{XSE} be used?

Best single-engine angle-of-climb speed will provide the maximum altitude gain in the shortest distance (steepest angle of climb). Use this speed when obstacles must be cleared with one engine out.

[PA.X.A, CA.X.A; FAA-H-8083-3]

19. In the event of an engine failure on takeoff, immediately before liftoff, what procedure is recommended?

Once the decision to reject a takeoff is made, the pilot should promptly close both throttles and maintain directional control with the rudder, nosewheel steering, and brakes. Aggressive use of rudder, nosewheel steering, and brakes may be required to keep the airplane on the runway. The primary objective is not necessarily to stop the airplane in the shortest distance, but to maintain control of the airplane as it decelerates.

[PA.IX.E, CA.IX.E; FAA-H-8083-3]

20. When practicing a simulated engine failure during takeoff, before reaching V_{MC}, the abort must be accomplished prior to reaching what speed?

The Airman Certification Standards note that "engine failure (simulated) during takeoff should be accomplished prior to reaching 50 percent of the calculated V_{MC}."

[PA.X.B, CA.X.B; FAA-S-ACS-6, FAA-S-ACS-7]

21. If engine failure occurs immediately after takeoff (airborne and gear down), what procedure is recommended?

If engine failure occurs prior to selecting the landing gear to the UP position, keep the nose as straight as possible, close both throttles, allow the nose to maintain airspeed, and descend to the runway. Concentrate on a normal landing and do not force the aircraft on the ground. Land on the remaining runway or overrun. Depending upon how quickly the pilot reacts to the sudden yaw, the airplane may run off the side of the runway by the time action is taken. The chances of maintaining directional control while retracting the flaps (if extended), landing gear, feathering the propeller, and accelerating are minimal. On some airplanes with a single engine-driven hydraulic pump, failure of that engine means the only way to raise the landing gear is to allow the engine to windmill or to use a hand pump. This is not a viable alternative during takeoff.

[PA.IX.F, CA.IX.F; FAA-H-8083-3]

22. If an engine failure occurs after takeoff (airborne and gear up), and climb performance is inadequate, what procedure is recommended?

When operating near or above the single-engine ceiling and an engine failure is experienced shortly after liftoff, a landing must be accomplished on essentially whatever lies ahead. There is also the option of continuing ahead, in a descent at V_{YSE} with the remaining engine producing power, as long as the pilot is not tempted to remain airborne beyond the airplane's performance capability. Remaining airborne, bleeding off airspeed in a futile attempt to maintain altitude, is almost invariably fatal. Landing under control is paramount. The greatest hazard in a single-engine takeoff is attempting to fly when it is not within the performance capability of the airplane to do so. An accident is inevitable.

[PA.IX.F, CA.IX.F; FAA-H-8083-3]

23. If an engine failure occurs immediately after takeoff (airborne and gear up) and climb performance is adequate, what are the four main areas of concern?

a. *Control*—The first priority is control of the airplane. Use aileron and rudder aggressively, if necessary, to counteract the yaw and roll from asymmetrical thrust.

b. *Configuration*—The memory items from the "engine failure after takeoff" checklist should be promptly executed to configure the airplane for climb.

c. *Climb*—As soon as directional control is established and the airplane configured for climb, the bank angle should be reduced to that producing best climb performance.

d. *Checklist*—Having accomplished the memory items from the "engine failure after takeoff" checklist, the printed copy should be reviewed as time permits. The "securing failed engine" checklist should then be accomplished.

[PA.IX.F, CA.IX.F; FAA-H-8083-3]

24. **Following an engine failure on takeoff (airborne) a climb cannot be established. What speed should be used to establish the slowest descent rate?**

When operating near or above the single-engine ceiling and an engine failure is experienced shortly after liftoff, V_{YSE} will deliver the least possible rate of sink (drift down).

[PA.IX.F, CA.IX.F; FAA-H-8083-3, FAA-P-8740-66]

25. **What are the two different sets of bank angles used to initially achieve directional control, and then to achieve climb performance, after an engine failure has occurred on departure?**

The two first bank angles a pilot must use initially include a bank angle and speed that avoids V_{MC} and establishes a zero sideslip flight condition. By applying the appropriate V_{MC} bank angle toward the operative engine, the pilot can counteract the yawing moment caused by the failed engine's asymmetric thrust, thereby maintaining directional control. The zero sideslip bank angle is used to counteract the sideslip or yaw caused by the failed engine's asymmetric thrust. By banking toward the operative engine, the pilot can eliminate or minimize the sideslip and maintain the aircraft's directional stability. Unlike the V_{MC} bank angle, the zero-sideslip bank angle is not a specific angle but rather a technique used to achieve coordinated flight after an engine failure.

[PA.IX.F, CA.IX.F; FAA-H-8083-3]

26. **To mitigate risk, what minimum airspeed and altitude is recommended when practicing a simulated engine failure after liftoff?**

Airman Certification Standards note that an "evaluator must not simulate failure of an engine until attaining an altitude of at least 400 feet AGL and at least minimum single-engine speed (V_{SSE}), best single-engine angle-of-climb speed (V_{XSE}), or best single-engine rate-of climb (V_{YSE})." The same suggestions would be recommended for practice.

[PA.IX.F, CA.IX.F; FAA-P-8740-66]

27. In the event of an engine failure immediately after takeoff, which is more important, more altitude or airspeed in excess of V$_{YSE}$ (single-engine best rate-of-climb speed)?

Altitude is more essential to safety after takeoff than is excess airspeed. Excess airspeed cannot be converted readily to the altitude, or the distance necessary to reach a landing area safely in the event of an emergency. In contrast, however, an airplane that has attained a safe altitude will fly in level flight much easier than it will climb. Therefore, if the total energy of both engines is initially used to gain enough height to clear all obstacles while in flight (safe maneuvering altitude), the problem is much simpler in the event an engine fails. If some extra height is available, it usually can be traded for velocity or gliding distance when needed.

[PA.IX.F, CA.IX.F; FAA-H-8083-3, FAA-P-8740-66]

28. If an engine fails immediately after takeoff, and you have already retracted the landing gear, how will you know whether to continue a single-engine climb or attempt a landing on the remaining runway?

When you are operating near or above the single-engine ceiling, and an engine failure is experienced shortly after lift-off, a landing needs to be accomplished on whatever essentially lies ahead. There is also the option of continuing ahead, in a descent at V$_{YSE}$ with the remaining engine producing power, as long as the pilot is not tempted to remain airborne beyond the airplane's performance capability. The gear should remain in the up selected position until the pilot has established a climb, and then returned to a position from which a landing will be made at which point the pilot then selects the gear to the down position. Putting the gear down may reduce critically needed climb ability when an engine failure is experienced right after takeoff. Analysis of engine failures on takeoff reveals a very high success rate of off-airport engine inoperative landings when the airplane is landed under control, even with the gear in the up position.

[PA.IX.F, CA.IX.F; FAA-H-8083-3]

29. Are the procedures you would follow for an enroute engine failure any different than those you would use for an engine failure at low altitude?

Engine failures well above the ground are handled differently than those occurring at lower speeds and altitudes. Cruise airspeed allows better airplane control and altitude, which may permit time for a possible diagnosis and remedy of the failure. Maintaining airplane control, however, is still paramount. If the condition cannot be corrected, the single-engine procedure recommended by the manufacturer should be accomplished and a landing made as soon as possible.

[PA.X.A, CA.X.A; FAA-H-8083-3]

30. What is the main problem when an engine fails en route?

When an engine fails en route during cruising flight, the pilot's main problem (after handling the emergency) is to maintain sufficient altitude to be able to continue flight to the nearest suitable airport and execute a safe landing. This is dependent upon density altitude, the gross weight of the airplane, and elevation of the terrain and obstructions. If the airplane is above its single-engine absolute ceiling at the time of engine failure, it will slowly lose altitude. The pilot should maintain V_{YSE} to minimize the rate of altitude loss.

[PA.X.A, CA.X.A; FAA-H-8083-3]

31. Describe some of the actions you might take when experiencing an engine failure while en route.

Many cases of power loss are related to fuel starvation, and restoration of power can be made by selecting another tank. An orderly inventory of gauges and switches may reveal the problem. Carburetor heat or alternate air can be selected. The affected engine may run smoothly on just one magneto or at a lower power setting. Altering the mixture might help. If fuel vapor formation is suspected, fuel boost pump operation may be used to eliminate flow and pressure fluctuations.

[PA.X.A, CA.X.A; FAA-H-8083-3]

32. If a pilot suspects a loss of power on a turbocharged engine has occurred at higher altitude, what remedy might the pilot consider to re-establish power?

A turbocharged aircraft will provide too much fuel in the air-fuel mixture to the engine at higher altitudes. If a turbocharger failure occurs at higher altitude, the pilot might be able to re-establish more power by leaning the mixture further and/or descending to a lower altitude where a normally aspirated engine (which the aircraft may then be operating as) will perform better.

[PA.X.A, CA.X.A; FAA-H-8083-3]

33. After feathering the propeller of a failed engine, what other actions must be accomplished to secure that engine?

Reference your aircraft's AFM. Normally, to completely secure an engine, you must turn off the fuel (mixture, electric boost pump, and fuel selector), ignition, and alternator/generator, and close the cowl flaps. Pressurized aircraft may have an air bleed to close for the failed engine.

[PA.X.A, CA.X.A; FAA-H-8083-3]

34. Explain the risks associated with an improper inflight restart of an inoperative engine that has been feathered.

Improper inflight restart of an inoperative engine might result in the following:

a. The restart and unfeathering of the propeller on an engine that was shut down for precautionary mechanical reasons could result in additional damage to the engine. An oil or fuel leak could become worse and cause a possible inflight fire.

b. During the attempted restart, the propeller could come out of feather using unfeathering accumulators or a starter, and the engine could fail to restart. If the propeller cannot be feathered again (propeller windmilling speed below start-lock disengagement speed), it will now be windmilling, resulting in significant drag and a loss of performance. The airplane will be unable to maintain level flight.

(continued)

c. When shutting down, securing, and restarting an engine for training purposes, consider that an improper restart might result in an engine that will not restart, creating an *actual* emergency.

Note: When restarting an inoperative engine, always follow the manufacturer's checklist and give consideration to all of the hazards associated with the procedure.

[PA.X.A, CA.X.A; SAIB CE-05-51]

35. In the event of an engine failure during the approach and landing phases of flight, what procedures are recommended?

a. The approach and landing with one engine inoperative is essentially the same as a two-engine approach and landing. The traffic pattern should be flown at similar altitudes, airspeeds, and key positions as in a two-engine approach.

b. With adequate airspeed and performance, the landing gear can still be extended on the downwind leg, in which case it should be confirmed DOWN no later than abeam the intended point of landing.

c. Performance permitting, initial extension of wing flaps (10°, typically) and a descent from pattern altitude can also be initiated on the downwind leg. The airspeed should be no slower than V_{YSE}.

d. On the base leg, if performance is adequate, the flaps may be extended to an intermediate setting (25°, typically). If the performance is inadequate, as measured by a decay in airspeed or high sink rate, delay further flap extension until closer to the runway. V_{YSE} is still the minimum airspeed to maintain.

e. On final approach, a normal, 3° glidepath to a landing is desirable. VASI or other vertical path lighting aids should be utilized if available. Slightly steeper approaches may be acceptable. However, a long, flat, low approach should be avoided. Large, sudden power applications or reductions should also be avoided. Maintain V_{YSE} until the landing is assured, then slow to 1.3 V_{S0} or the POH/AFM recommended speed. The final flap setting may be delayed until the landing is assured, or the airplane may be landed with partial flaps.

[PA.IX.G, CA.IX.G; FAA-H-8083-3]

36. When should the landing gear/flaps be extended prior to landing with one engine inoperative?

A best practice for pilots who might need to conduct a landing with one engine failed is to have the aircraft configured and established prior to reaching a final approach fix if on an instrument approach, or if flying a VFR approach to do so on the downwind leg during the pattern procedure. This allows the pilot to stabilize the aircraft, reduces V_{MC} effects (even if also reducing some performance), and allows the pilot the ability to focus on flying the single-engine approach.

[PA.IX.G, CA.IX.G; FAA-H-8083-3]

37. Are single-engine go-arounds recommended? Why?

Single-engine go-arounds must be avoided. As a practical matter in single-engine approaches, once the airplane is on final approach with landing gear and flaps extended, it is committed to land—if not on the intended runway, then on another runway, a taxiway, or a grassy infield. The light twin does not have the performance to climb on one engine with landing gear and flaps extended. Considerable altitude will be lost while maintaining V_{YSE} and retracting landing gear and flaps. Losses of 500 feet or more are not unusual. If the landing gear has been lowered with an alternate means of extension, retraction may not be possible, virtually negating any climb capability.

Exam Tip: For OEI flight, know the following bank angles for your airplane and when to fly them:

- 5 to 10 degrees of bank to initially assist the rudder in maintaining directional control in the event of an engine failure, as the pitch attitude for V_{YSE} is established.
- A 5-degree bank during the V_{MC} demonstration is required for the practical test for a multi-engine class rating.
- Approximately 2 to 3 degrees of bank with the ball slightly displaced toward the operative engine to achieve zero sideslip for best climb performance at V_{YSE}.

[PA.IV.N, CA.IV.N; FAA-H-8083-3]

38. **When performing a go-around procedure, which should be retracted first, the landing gear or the flaps?**

After establishing the proper climb attitude and power settings, the pilot's next concern is flap retraction. After the descent has been stopped, the landing flaps are partially retracted or placed in the takeoff position as recommended by the manufacturer. Depending on the airplane's altitude and airspeed, it is wise to retract the flaps intermittently in small increments to allow time for the airplane to accelerate progressively as they are being raised. A sudden and complete retraction of the flaps could cause a loss of lift, resulting in the airplane settling into the ground.

Unless otherwise specified in the AFM/POH, it is generally recommended that the flaps be retracted (at least partially) before retracting the landing gear for two reasons. First, on most airplanes, full flaps produce more drag than the landing gear. Second, in case the airplane inadvertently touches down as the go-around is initiated, it is desirable to have the landing gear in the down-and-locked position. After a positive rate of climb is established, the landing gear is retracted.

The landing gear is retracted only after the initial or rough trim is accomplished and when it is certain the airplane will remain airborne. During the initial part of an extremely low go-around, it is possible for the airplane to settle onto the runway and bounce. This situation is not particularly dangerous provided the airplane is kept straight and a constant, safe pitch attitude is maintained. With the application of power, the airplane attains a safe flying speed rapidly and the advanced power cushions any secondary touchdown.

[PA.IV.N, CA.IV.N; FAA-H-8083-3]

Multi-Engine
Maneuvers

4

The following excerpted multi-engine-specific maneuvers are in the Private and Commercial Airman Certification Standards (ACS) that a pilot will be required to demonstrate during a practical test. While tolerance standards may be slightly more stringent for demonstrations at the Commercial Pilot level of testing, nearly all of the required maneuvers are the same with the exception of the additional requirement to demonstrate an accelerated stall for a commercial pilot. Applicants are encouraged to review the general flow of the maneuvers here but also to reference the appropriate ACS for each maneuver as they prepare for testing.

This list is not inclusive of all ACS tasks but is a list of highlighted maneuvers that are of direct relevance to multi-engine flight operations.

A. Taxiing

1. Receive and correctly read back clearances/instructions, if applicable.

2. Use an airport diagram or taxi chart during taxi, if published, and maintain situational awareness.

3. Position the flight controls for the existing wind conditions.

4. Complete the appropriate checklist.

5. Perform a brake check immediately after the airplane begins moving.

6. Maintain positive control of the airplane during ground operations by controlling direction and speed without excessive use of brakes.

7. Comply with airport/taxiway markings, signals, and ATC clearances and instructions.

8. Position the airplane properly relative to hold lines.

Risk Management

Be prepared to identify, assess, and mitigate risks associated with:

1. Inappropriate activities and distractions.

2. Confirmation or expectation bias as related to taxi instructions.

3. A taxi route or departure runway change.

4. Runway incursion.

Exam Tip: Remember to perform a passenger briefing prior to taxi.

[PA.II.D, CA.II.D; FAA-H-8083-2, FAA-H-8083-3, FAA-H-8083-25, POH/AFM, AC 91-73, Chart Supplements, AIM]

B. Before Takeoff Check

1. Review takeoff performance.

2. Complete the appropriate checklist.

3. Position the airplane appropriately considering wind direction and the presence of any aircraft, vessels, or buildings as applicable.

4. Divide attention inside and outside the flight deck.

5. Verify that engine parameters and airplane configuration are suitable.

Risk Management

Be prepared to identify, assess, and mitigate risks associated with:

1. Division of attention while conducting preflight checks.

2. Unexpected runway changes by ATC.

3. Wake turbulence.

4. Potential powerplant failure during takeoff or other malfunction considering operational factors such as airplane characteristics, runway/takeoff path length, surface conditions, environmental conditions, and obstructions.

[PA.II.F, CA.II.F; FAA-H-8083-2, FAA-H-8083-3, FAA-H-8083-25, POH/AFM]

C. Normal Takeoff and Climb

Note: If a crosswind condition does not exist, the applicant's knowledge of crosswind elements must be evaluated through oral testing.

1. Complete the appropriate checklist.

2. Make radio calls as appropriate.

3. Verify assigned/correct runway.

4. Determine wind direction with or without visible wind direction indicators.

5. Position the flight controls for the existing wind conditions.

6. Clear the area, taxi into takeoff position, and align the airplane on the runway centerline.

(continued)

7. Advance the throttle smoothly to takeoff power and confirm proper engine and flight instrument indications prior to rotation.

8. Rotate and lift off at the recommended airspeed and accelerate to V_Y.

9. Establish a pitch attitude to maintain the manufacturer's recommended speed or V_Y, +10/−5 knots (Private) or ±5 knots (Commercial).

10. Configure the airplane in accordance with manufacturer's guidance.

11. Maintain V_Y, +10/−5 knots (Private) or ±5 knots (Commercial), to a safe maneuvering altitude.

12. Maintain directional control and proper wind-drift correction throughout takeoff and climb.

13. Comply with noise abatement procedures.

Risk Management
Be prepared to identify, assess, and mitigate risks associated with:

1. Selection of runway based on airplane performance and limitations, available distance, and wind.

2. Effects of crosswind, wind shear, tailwind, wake turbulence, and runway surface/conditions.

3. Abnormal operations, including planning for a rejected takeoff and a potential engine failure in the takeoff/climb phase of flight.

4. Collision hazards (e.g., aircraft, terrain, obstacles, wires, vehicles, vessels, persons, and wildlife).

5. Low-altitude maneuvering, including stall, spin, or controlled flight into terrain (CFIT).

6. Distractions, task prioritization, loss of situational awareness, or disorientation.

7. Runway incursion.

[PA.IV.A, CA.IV.A; FAA-H-8083-2, FAA-H-8083-3, POH/AFM, AIM]

D. Normal Approach and Landing

Note: If a crosswind condition does not exist, the applicant's knowledge of crosswind elements must be evaluated through oral testing.

1. Complete the appropriate checklist(s).

2. Make radio calls as appropriate.

3. Ensure the airplane is aligned with the correct/assigned runway or landing surface.

4. Scan the runway or landing surface and the adjoining area for traffic and obstructions.

5. Select and aim for a suitable touchdown point considering the wind conditions, landing surface, and obstructions.

6. Establish the recommended approach and landing configuration, airspeed, and trim, and adjust pitch attitude and power as required to maintain a stabilized approach.

7. Maintain manufacturer's published approach airspeed or in its absence not more than 1.3 times the stalling speed or the minimum steady flight speed in the landing configuration (V_{S0}), +10/−5 knots (Private) or ±5 knots (Commercial) with gust factor applied.

8. Maintain directional control and appropriate crosswind correction throughout the approach and landing.

9. Make smooth, timely, and correct control application during round out and touchdown.

10. Touch down at a proper pitch attitude, within 400 feet (Private) or 200 feet (Commercial) beyond or on the specified point, with no side drift, and with the airplane's longitudinal axis aligned with and over the runway center/landing path.

11. Execute a timely go-around if the approach cannot be made within the tolerances specified above or for any other condition that may result in an unsafe approach or landing.

12. Use runway incursion avoidance procedures, if applicable.

(continued)

Risk Management

Be prepared to identify, assess, and mitigate risks associated with:

1. Selection of runway/landing surface, approach path, and touchdown area based on pilot capability, airplane performance and limitations, available distance, and wind.

2. Effects of crosswind, wind shear, tailwind, wake turbulence, and runway surface/conditions.

3. Planning for a rejected landing and go-around and for land and hold short operations (LAHSO).

4. Collision hazards (e.g., aircraft, terrain, obstacles, wires, vehicles, vessels, persons, and wildlife).

5. Low-altitude maneuvering, including stall, spin, or CFIT.

6. Distractions, task prioritization, loss of situational awareness, or disorientation.

[PA.IV.B, CA.IV.B; FAA-H-8083-2, FAA-H-8083-3, FAA-H-8083-25, POH/AFM, AIM]

E. Short-Field Takeoff and Maximum Performance Climb

1. Complete the appropriate checklist.

2. Make radio calls as appropriate.

3. Verify assigned/correct runway.

4. Determine wind direction with or without visible wind direction indicators.

5. Position the flight controls for the existing wind, if applicable.

6. Clear the area, taxi into takeoff position, and align the airplane on the runway centerline utilizing maximum available takeoff area.

7. Apply brakes while setting engine power to achieve maximum performance.

8. Confirm takeoff power prior to brake release and verify proper engine and flight instrument indications prior to rotation.

9. Rotate and lift off at the recommended airspeed and accelerate to the recommended obstacle clearance airspeed or V_X, +10/−5 knots (Private) or ±5 knots (Commercial).

10. Establish a pitch attitude to maintain the recommended obstacle clearance airspeed or V_X, +10/−5 knots (Private) or ±5 knots (Commercial), until the obstacle is cleared or until the airplane is 50 feet above the surface.

11. Establish a pitch attitude for V_Y and accelerate to V_Y +10/−5 knots (Private) or ±5 knots (Commercial) after clearing the obstacle or at 50 feet AGL if simulating an obstacle.

12. Configure the airplane in accordance with the manufacturer's guidance after a positive rate of climb has been verified.

13. Maintain V_Y +10/−5 knots (Private) or ±5 knots (Commercial) to a safe maneuvering altitude.

14. Maintain directional control and proper wind-drift correction throughout takeoff and climb.

15. Comply with noise abatement procedures.

Risk Management
Be prepared to identify, assess and mitigate risks associated with:

1. Selection of runway based on pilot capability, airplane performance and limitations, available distance, and wind.

2. Effects of crosswind, wind shear, tailwind, wake turbulence, and runway surface/condition.

3. Abnormal operations, including planning for a rejected takeoff and a potential engine failure in the takeoff/climb phase of flight.

4. Collision hazards (e.g., aircraft, terrain, obstacles, wires, vehicles, persons, and wildlife).

5. Low-altitude maneuvering, including stall, spin, or CFIT.

6. Distractions, task prioritization, loss of situational awareness, or disorientation.

[PA.IV.E, CA.IV.E; FAA-H-8083-2, FAA-H-8083-3, FAA-H-8083-25, POH/AFM, AIM]

F. Short-Field Approach and Landing

1. Complete the appropriate checklist.

2. Make radio calls as appropriate.

3. Ensure the airplane is aligned with the correct/assigned runway.

4. Scan the landing runway and adjoining area for traffic and obstructions.

5. Select and aim for a suitable touchdown point considering the wind conditions, landing surface, and obstructions.

6. Establish the recommended approach and landing configuration, airspeed, and trim, and adjust pitch attitude and power as required to maintain a stabilized approach.

7. Maintain manufacturer's published approach airspeed or in its absence not more than 1.3 V_{S0}, +10/−5 knots (Private) or ±5 knots (Commercial) with gust factor applied.

8. Maintain directional control and appropriate crosswind correction throughout the approach and landing.

9. Make smooth, timely, and correct control application before, during, and after touchdown.

10. Touch down at a proper pitch attitude within 200 feet (Private) or 100 feet (Commercial) beyond or on the specified point, threshold markings, or runway numbers, with no side drift, minimum float, and with the airplane's longitudinal axis aligned with and over the runway centerline.

11. Use manufacturer's recommended procedures for airplane configuration and braking.

12. Execute a timely go-around if the approach cannot be made within the tolerances specified above or for any other condition that may result in an unsafe approach or landing.

13. Utilize runway incursion avoidance procedures.

Risk Management
Be prepared to identify, assess, and mitigate risks associated with:

1. Selection of runway based on pilot capability, airplane performance and limitations, available distance, and wind.

2. Effects of crosswind, wind shear, tailwind, wake turbulence, and landing surface/condition.

3. Planning for a rejected landing and go-around and for land and hold short operations (LAHSO).

4. Collision hazards (e.g., aircraft, terrain, obstacles, wires, vehicles, persons, and wildlife).

5. Low-altitude maneuvering, including stall, spin, or CFIT.

6. Distractions, task prioritization, loss of situational awareness, or disorientation.

[PA.IV.F, CA.IV.F; FAA-H-8083-2, FAA-H-8083-3, POH/AFM, AIM]

G. Go-Around/Rejected Landing

1. Complete the appropriate checklist.

2. Make radio calls as appropriate.

3. Make a timely decision to discontinue the approach to landing.

4. Apply takeoff power immediately and transition to climb pitch attitude for V_X or V_Y as appropriate +10/−5 knots (Private) or ±5 knots (Commercial).

5. Configure the airplane after a positive rate of climb has been verified or in accordance with airplane manufacturer's instructions.

6. Maneuver to the side of the runway/landing area when necessary to clear and avoid conflicting traffic.

7. Maintain V_Y +10/−5 knots (Private) or ±5 knots (Commercial) to a safe maneuvering altitude

8. Maintain directional control and proper wind-drift correction throughout the climb.

9. Use runway incursion avoidance procedures, if applicable.

Risk Management
Be prepared to identify, assess, and mitigate risks associated with:

1. Delayed recognition of the need for a go-around/rejected landing.

2. Delayed performance of a go-around at low altitude

3. Power application.

4. Configuring the airplane.

(continued)

5. Collision hazards (e.g., aircraft, terrain, obstacles, wires, vehicles, vessels, persons, and wildlife).

6. Low-altitude maneuvering, including, stall, spin, or CFIT.

7. Distractions, task prioritization, loss of situational awareness, or disorientation.

8. Runway incursion.

9. Managing a go-around/rejected landing after accepting a LAHSO clearance.

Exam Tip: Note that this maneuver is not indicated or intended to be evaluated in a single-engine, or engine failed configuration. While a go-around is commonly tested on single-engine Private and Commercial practical tests, it is less commonly focused on as a maneuver that is additionally potentially selected for demonstration in a multi-engine practical test.

[PA.IV.N, CA.IV.N; FAA-H-8083-2, FAA-H-8083-3, FAA-H-8083-25, POH/AFM, AIM]

H. Steep Turns

1. Clear the area.

2. Establish the manufacturer's recommended airspeed, or if one is not available, an airspeed not to exceed the maneuvering speed (V_A).

3. Roll into a coordinated 360° steep turn with approximately a 45° bank (Private) or 50° bank (Commercial).

4. Perform the task in the opposite direction, as specified by evaluator.

5. Maintain the entry altitude ±100 feet, airspeed ±10 knots, bank ±5°, and roll out on the entry heading ±10°.

Risk Management
Be prepared to identify, assess, and mitigate risks associated with:

1. Division of attention between aircraft control and orientation.

2. Collision hazards (e.g., aircraft, terrain, obstacles, and wires).

3. Low-altitude maneuvering, including stall, spin, or CFIT.

4. Distractions, task prioritization, loss of situational awareness, or disorientation.

5. Uncoordinated flight.

Exam Tip: Remember to always perform "clearing turns" prior to any maneuver.

[PA.V.A, CA.V.A; FAA-H-8083-2, FAA-H-8083-3, FAA-H-8083-25, POH/AFM]

I. Maneuvering During Slow Flight

Note: Evaluation criteria for this task should recognize that environmental factors (e.g., turbulence) may result in a momentary activation of stall warning indicators such as the stall horn. If the applicant recognizes the stall warning indication and promptly makes an appropriate correction, a momentary activation does not constitute unsatisfactory performance on this task. As with other tasks, unsatisfactory performance would arise from an applicant's continual deviation from the standard, lack of correction, and/or lack of recognition.

1. Clear the area.

2. Select an entry altitude that allows the task to be completed no lower than 3,000 feet AGL.

3. Establish and maintain an airspeed at which any further increase in angle of attack, increase in load factor, or reduction in power would result in a stall warning (e.g., aircraft buffet, stall horn, etc.).

4. Accomplish coordinated straight-and-level flight, turns, climbs, and descents with the aircraft configured as specified by the evaluator without a stall warning (e.g., aircraft buffet, stall horn, etc.).

5. Maintain the specified altitude, ±100 feet (Private) or ±50 feet (Commercial); specified heading, ±10°; airspeed, +10/−0 knots (Private) or +5/−0 knots (Commercial); and specified angle of bank, ±10° (Private) or ±5° (Commercial).

Risk Management
Be prepared to identify, assess, and mitigate risks associated with:

1. Inadvertent slow flight and flight with a stall warning, which could lead to loss of control.

(continued)

2. Range and limitations of stall warning indicators (e.g., aircraft buffet, stall horn, etc.).

3. Uncoordinated flight.

4. Effect of environmental elements on airplane performance (e.g., turbulence, microbursts, and high density altitude).

5. Collision hazards (e.g., aircraft, terrain, obstacles, and wires).

6. Distractions, task prioritization, loss of situational awareness, or disorientation.

[PA.VII.A, CA.VII.A; FAA-H-8083-2, FAA-H-8083-3, FAA-H-8083-25, POH/AFM]

J. Power-Off Stalls

Note: Evaluation criteria for a recovery from an approach to stall should not mandate a predetermined value for altitude loss and should not mandate maintaining altitude during recovery. Proper evaluation criteria should consider the multitude of external and internal variables that affect the recovery altitude.

1. Clear the area.

2. Select an entry altitude that allows the task to be completed no lower than 3,000 feet AGL.

3. Configure the airplane in the approach or landing configuration, as specified by the evaluator, and maintain coordinated flight throughout the maneuver.

4. Establish a stabilized descent.

5. Transition smoothly from the approach or landing attitude to a pitch attitude that induces a stall.

6. Maintain a specified heading, ±10° if in straight flight; maintain a specified angle of bank not to exceed 20°, ±10° (Private) or ±5° (Commercial) if in turning flight, while inducing the stall.

7. Acknowledge cues of the impending stall and then recover promptly after a full stall occurs.

8. Execute a stall recovery in accordance with procedures set forth in the POH or AFM.

9. Configure the airplane as recommended by the manufacturer, and accelerate to best angle of climb speed (V_X) or best rate of climb speed (V_Y).

10. Return to the altitude, heading, and airspeed specified by the evaluator.

11. Use single-pilot resource management (SRM) or crew resource management (CRM), as appropriate.

Risk Management
Be prepared to identify, assess, and mitigate risks associated with:

1. Factors and situations that could lead to an inadvertent power-off stall, spin, and loss of control.

2. Range and limitations of stall warning indicators (e.g., airplane buffet, stall horn, etc.).

3. Stall warning(s) during normal operations.

4. Stall recovery procedure.

5. Secondary stalls, accelerated stalls, and cross-control stalls.

6. Effect of environmental elements on airplane performance related to power-off stalls (e.g., turbulence, microbursts, and high density altitude).

7. Collision hazards (e.g., aircraft, terrain, obstacles, and wires).

8. Distractions, task prioritization, loss of situational awareness, or disorientation.

[PA.VII.B, CA.VII.B; FAA-H-8083-2, FAA-H-8083-3, FAA-H-8083-25, AC 61-67, POH/AFM]

K. Power-On Stalls

Note: In some high-performance airplanes, the power setting may have to be reduced below the ACS guidelines to prevent excessively high pitch attitudes greater than 30° nose up. Evaluation criteria for a recovery from an approach to stall should not mandate a predetermined value for altitude loss and should not mandate maintaining altitude during recovery. Proper evaluation criteria should consider the multitude of external and internal variables that affect the recovery altitude.

1. Clear the area.

2. Select an entry altitude that allows the task to be completed no lower than 3,000 feet AGL.

3. Establish the takeoff, departure, or cruise configuration, as specified by the evaluator, and maintain coordinated flight throughout the maneuver.

4. Set power (as assigned by the evaluator) to no less than 65 percent power.

5. Transition smoothly from the takeoff or departure attitude to the pitch attitude that induces a stall.

6. Maintain a specified heading, ±10° if in straight flight; maintain a specified angle of bank not to exceed 20°, ±10° if in turning flight, while inducing the stall (Private) or until an impending or full stall is reached, as specified by the evaluator (Commercial).

7. Acknowledge cues of the impending stall and then recover promptly after a full stall occurs (Private), or acknowledge the cues at the first indication of a stall (Commercial).

8. Execute a stall recovery in accordance with procedures set forth in the POH/AFM (Private), or recover at the first indication of a stall or after a full stall has occurred, as specified by the evaluator (Commercial).

9. Configure the airplane as recommended by the manufacturer, and accelerate to V_X or V_Y.

10. Return to the altitude, heading, and airspeed specified by the evaluator.

11. Use single-pilot resource management (SRM) or crew resource management (CRM), as appropriate.

Risk Management

Be prepared to identify, assess, and mitigate risks associated with:

1. Factors and situations that could lead to an inadvertent power-on stall, spin, and loss of control.

2. Range and limitations of stall warning indicators (e.g., aircraft buffet, stall horn, etc.).

3. Stall warning(s) during normal operations.

4. Stall recovery procedure.

5. Secondary stalls, accelerated stalls, elevator trim stalls, and cross-control stalls.

6. Effect of environmental elements on airplane performance related to power-on stalls (e.g., turbulence, microbursts, and high density altitude).

7. Collision hazards (e.g., aircraft, terrain, obstacles, and wires).

8. Distractions, task prioritization, loss of situational awareness, or disorientation.

[PA.VII.C, CA.VII.C; FAA-H-8083-2, FAA-H-8083-3, FAA-H-8083-25, AC 61-67, POH/AFM]

L. Accelerated Stalls (Commercial Pilots Only)

1. Clear the area.

2. Select an entry altitude that allows the Task to be completed no lower than 3,000 feet AGL.

3. Establish the configuration as specified by the evaluator.

4. Set power appropriate for the configuration, such that the airspeed does not exceed the maneuvering speed (V_A) or any other applicable POH/AFM limitation.

5. Establish and maintain a coordinated turn in a 45° bank, increasing elevator back pressure smoothly and firmly until an impending stall is reached.

6. Acknowledge the cues at the first indication of a stall (e.g., aircraft buffet, stall horn, etc.).

(continued)

7. Execute a stall recovery in accordance with procedures set forth in the POH/AFM.

8. Configure the airplane as recommended by the manufacturer, and accelerate to V_X or V_Y.

9. Return to the altitude, heading, and airspeed specified by the evaluator.

Risk Management
Be prepared to identify, assess, and mitigate risks associated with:

1. Factors and situations that could lead to an inadvertent accelerated stall, spin, and loss of control.

2. Range and limitations of stall warning indicators (e.g., aircraft buffet, stall horn, etc.).

3. Stall warning(s) during normal operations.

4. Stall recovery procedure.

5. Secondary stalls, cross-control stalls, and spins.

6. Effect of environmental elements on airplane performance related to accelerated stalls (e.g., turbulence, microbursts, and high density altitude).

7. Collision hazards (e.g., aircraft, terrain, obstacles, and wires).

8. Distractions, task prioritization, loss of situational awareness, or disorientation.

[CA.VII.D; FAA-H-8083-2, FAA-H-8083-3, FAA-H-8083-25, AC 61-67, POH/AFM]

M. Supplemental Oxygen

1. Determine the quantity of supplemental oxygen required in a scenario given by the evaluator.

2. Operate or simulate operation of the installed or portable oxygen equipment in the airplane, if installed or available.

3. Brief passengers on use of supplemental oxygen equipment in a scenario given by the evaluator.

4. Use single-pilot resource management (SRM) or crew resource management (CRM), as appropriate.

Risk Management
Be prepared to identify, assess, and mitigate risks associated with:

1. High altitude flight.

2. Use of supplemental oxygen.

3. Management of compressed gas containers.

4. Combustion hazards in an oxygen-rich environment.

[PA.I.G, CA.VIII.A; FAA-H-8083-2, FAA-H-8083-3, FAA-H-8083-25, 14 CFR Part 91, AC 61-107, POH/AFM]

N. Pressurization

1. Operate the pressurization system, if equipment is installed.

2. Respond appropriately to simulated pressurization malfunctions, if equipment is installed.

3. Brief passengers on use of supplemental oxygen in the case of pressurization malfunction, if equipment is installed.

4. Use single-pilot resource management (SRM) or crew resource management (CRM), as appropriate.

Risk Management
Be prepared to identify, assess, and mitigate risks associated with:

1. High altitude flight.

2. Malfunction of pressurization system, if equipment is installed.

[CA.VIII.B; FAA-H-8083-2, FAA-H-8083-3, POH/AFM]

O. Emergency Descent

1. Clear the area.

2. Establish and maintain the appropriate airspeed and configuration appropriate to the scenario specified by the evaluator and as covered in POH/AFM for the emergency descent.

3. Maintain orientation, divide attention appropriately, and plan and execute a smooth recovery.

4. Use bank angle between 30° and 45° to maintain positive load factors during the descent.

(continued)

5. Maintain appropriate airspeed, +0/−10 knots, and level off at a specified altitude, ±100 feet.

6. Complete the appropriate checklist(s).

7. Make radio calls as appropriate.

8. Use single-pilot resource management (SRM) or crew resource management (CRM), as appropriate.

Risk Management
Be prepared to identify, assess, and mitigate risks associated with:

1. Altitude, wind, terrain, obstructions, gliding distance, and available landing distance considerations.

2. Collision hazards (e.g., aircraft, terrain, obstacles, and wires).

3. Configuring the airplane.

4. Distractions, task prioritization, loss of situational awareness, or disorientation.

[PA.IX.A, CA.IX.A; FAA-H-8083-2, FAA-H-8083-3, FAA-H-8083-25, POH/AFM]

P. Engine Failure During Takeoff Before V_{MC} (Simulated)

1. Close the throttles smoothly and promptly when a simulated engine failure occurs.

2. Maintain directional control and apply brakes, as necessary.

Note: Engine failure (simulated) during takeoff should be accomplished prior to reaching 50 percent of the calculated V_{MC}.

Risk Management
Be prepared to identify, assess, and mitigate risks associated with:

1. Potential engine failure during takeoff.

2. Configuring the airplane.

3. Distractions, task prioritization, loss of situational awareness, or disorientation.

[PA.IX.E, CA.IX.E; FAA-H-8083-2, FAA-H-8083-3, FAA-H-8083-25, FAA-P-8740-66, POH/AFM]

Q. Engine Failure After Liftoff (Simulated)

1. Promptly recognize an engine failure, maintain control, and utilize appropriate emergency procedures.

2. Establish V_{YSE}; if obstructions are present, establish V_{XSE} or V_{MC} +5 knots, whichever is greater, until obstructions are cleared. Then transition to V_{YSE}.

3. Reduce drag by retracting landing gear and flaps in accordance with the manufacturer's guidance.

4. Simulate feathering the propeller on the inoperative engine (evaluator should then establish zero thrust on the inoperative engine).

5. Use flight controls in the proper combination as recommended by the manufacturer, or as required to maintain best performance, and trim as required.

6. Monitor the operating engine and aircraft systems and make adjustments as necessary.

7. Recognize the airplane's performance capabilities. If a climb is not possible at V_{YSE}, maintain V_{YSE} and return to the departure airport for landing, or initiate an approach to the most suitable landing area available.

8. Simulate securing the inoperative engine.

9. Maintain heading ±10° and airspeed ±5 knots.

10. Complete the appropriate checklist(s).

Risk Management
Be prepared to identify, assess, and mitigate risks associated with:

1. Potential engine failure after liftoff.

2. Collision hazards (e.g., aircraft, terrain, obstacles, and wires).

3. Configuring the airplane.

4. Low-altitude maneuvering, including stall, spin, or CFIT.

5. Distractions, task prioritization, loss of situational awareness, or disorientation.

Note: On multi-engine practical tests, where the failure of the most critical engine after liftoff is required, the evaluator must consider local atmospheric conditions, terrain, and type of aircraft used.

(continued)

The evaluator must not simulate failure of an engine until attaining at least $V_{SSE}/V_{XSE}/V_{YSE}$ and an altitude not lower than 400 feet AGL.

[PA.IX.F, CA.IX.F; FAA-H-8083-2, FAA-H-8083-3, FAA-H-8083-25, FAA-P-8740-66, POH/AFM]

R. Approach and Landing with an Inoperative Engine (Simulated)

1. Promptly recognize an engine failure and maintain positive airplane control.

2. Set the engine controls, reduce drag, identify and verify the inoperative engine, and simulate feathering of the propeller on the inoperative engine. (Evaluator should then establish zero thrust on the inoperative engine.)

3. Use flight controls in the proper combination as recommended by the manufacturer or as required to maintain best performance, and trim as required.

4. Follow the manufacturer's recommended emergency procedures and complete the appropriate checklist.

5. Monitor the operating engine and aircraft systems and make adjustments as necessary.

6. Maintain the manufacturer's recommended approach airspeed +10/−5 knots (Private) or ±5 knots (Commercial) in the landing configuration with a stabilized approach, until landing is assured.

7. Make smooth, timely, and correct control applications before, during, and after touchdown.

8. Touch down on the first one-third of available runway/landing surface, with no drift, and the airplane's longitudinal axis aligned with and over the runway center or landing path.

9. Maintain directional control and appropriate crosswind correction throughout the approach and landing.

10. Complete the appropriate checklist(s).

Risk Management

Be prepared to identify, assess, and mitigate risks associated with:

1. Potential engine failure in flight or during an approach.

2. Collision hazards (e.g., aircraft, terrain, obstacles, and wires).

3. Configuring the airplane.

4. Low-altitude maneuvering, including stall, spin, or CFIT.

5. Distractions, task prioritization, loss of situational awareness, or disorientation.

6. Possible single-engine go-around.

[PA.IX.G, CA.IX.G; FAA-H-8083-2, FAA-H-8083-3, FAA-H-8083-25, FAA-P-8740-66, POH/AFM]

S. Maneuvering with One Engine Inoperative

1. Recognize an engine failure, maintain control, use the manufacturer's memory item procedures, and use appropriate emergency procedures.

2. Set the engine controls, identify and verify the inoperative engine, and feather the appropriate propeller.

3. Use flight controls in the proper combination as recommended by the manufacturer, or as required to maintain best performance, and trim as required.

4. Attempt to determine and resolve the reason for the engine failure.

5. Secure the inoperative engine and monitor the operating engine and make necessary adjustments.

6. Restart the inoperative engine using the manufacturer's restart procedures.

7. Maintain altitude ±100 feet, or minimum sink rate if applicable; airspeed ±10 knots; and selected headings ±10°.

8. Complete the appropriate checklist(s).

Note: For safety reasons, when the practical test is conducted in an airplane, the applicant must perform tasks that require feathering or shutdown only under conditions and at a position and altitude

(continued)

where it is possible to make a safe landing on an established airport if there is difficulty in unfeathering the propeller or restarting the engine. The evaluator must select an entry altitude that will allow the single-engine demonstration tasks to be completed no lower than 3,000 feet AGL or the manufacturer's recommended altitude (whichever is higher). If it is not possible to unfeather the propeller or restart the engine while airborne, the applicant and the evaluator should treat the situation as an emergency. At altitudes lower than 3,000 feet AGL, engine failure should be simulated by reducing throttle to idle and then establishing zero thrust.

Risk Management
Be prepared to identify, assess, and mitigate risks associated with:

1. Potential engine failure during flight.
2. Collision hazards (e.g., aircraft, terrain, obstacles, and wires).
3. Configuring the airplane.
4. Low-altitude maneuvering including stall, spin, or CFIT.
5. Distractions, task prioritization, loss of situational awareness, or disorientation.

[PA.X.A, CA.X.A; FAA-H-8083-2, FAA-H-8083-3, FAA-H-8083-25, FAA-P-8740-66, POH/AFM]

T. V_{MC} Demonstration

1. Configure the airplane in accordance with the manufacturer's recommendations. In the absence of the manufacturer's recommendations, then at safe single-engine speed (V_{SSE}/V_{YSE}), as appropriate, and:
   a. Landing gear retracted.
   b. Flaps set for takeoff.
   c. Cowl flaps set for takeoff.
   d. Trim set for takeoff.
   e. Propellers set for high RPM.
   f. Power on critical engine reduced to idle and propeller windmilling.
   g. Power on operating engine set to takeoff or maximum available power.

2. Establish a single-engine climb attitude with the airspeed at approximately 10 knots above V_{SSE}.

3. Establish a bank angle not to exceed 5° toward the operating engine, as required for best performance and controllability.

4. Increase the pitch attitude slowly to reduce the airspeed at approximately 1 knot per second while applying increased rudder pressure as needed to maintain directional control.

5. Recognize and recover at the first indication of loss of directional control, stall warning, or buffet.

6. Recover promptly by simultaneously reducing power sufficiently on the operating engine, decreasing the angle of attack as necessary to regain airspeed and directional control, and without adding power on the simulated failed engine.

7. Recover within 20° of entry heading.

8. Advance power smoothly on the operating engine and accelerate to $V_{SSE}/V_{YSE,}$ as appropriate, +10/−5 knots (Private) or ±5 knots (Commercial) during recovery.

Risk Management
Be prepared to identify, assess, and mitigate risks associated with:

1. Configuring the airplane.

2. Maneuvering with one engine inoperative.

3. Distractions, task prioritization, loss of situational awareness, or disorientation.

Note: Airplanes with normally aspirated engines will lose power as altitude increases because of the reduced density of the air entering the induction system of the engine. This loss of power will result in a V_{MC} lower than the stall speed at higher altitudes. Therefore, recovery should be made at the first indication of loss of directional control, stall warning, or buffet. Do not perform this maneuver by increasing the pitch attitude to a high angle with both engines operating and then reducing power on the critical engine. This technique is hazardous and may result in loss of airplane control.

[PA.X.B, CA.X.B; FAA-H-8083-2, FAA-H-8083-3, FAA-H-8083-25, FAA-P-8740-66, POH/AFM]

U. One Engine Inoperative (Simulated) (solely by Reference to Instruments) During Straight-and-Level Flight and Turns

1. Promptly recognize an engine failure and maintain positive airplane control.

2. Set the engine controls, reduce drag, identify and verify the inoperative engine, and simulate feathering of the propeller on the inoperative engine. (Evaluator should then establish zero thrust on the inoperative engine.)

3. Establish the best engine-inoperative airspeed and trim the airplane.

4. Use flight controls in the proper combination as recommended by the manufacturer, or as required to maintain best performance, and trim as required.

5. Verify the prescribed checklist procedures used for securing the inoperative engine.

6. Attempt to determine and resolve the reason for the engine failure.

7. Monitor engine functions and make necessary adjustments.

8. Maintain the specified altitude ±100 feet, or minimum sink rate if applicable; airspeed ±10 knots; and the specified heading ±10°.

9. Assess the airplane's performance capability and decide an appropriate action to ensure a safe landing.

10. Avoid loss of airplane control or attempted flight contrary to the engine-inoperative operating limitations of the airplane.

11. Use single-pilot resource management (SRM) or crew resource management (CRM), as appropriate.

Risk Management
Be prepared to identify, assess, and mitigate risks associated with:

1. Identification of the inoperative engine.

2. Inability to climb or maintain altitude with an inoperative engine.

3. Low-altitude maneuvering including stall, spin, or CFIT.

4. Distractions, task prioritization, loss of situational awareness, or disorientation.

5. Fuel management during single-engine operation.

Note: If you do not hold an Instrument–Airplane Rating, this task is not required.

[PA.X.C, CA.X.C; FAA-H-8083-2, FAA-H-8083-3, FAA-H-8083-15, FAA-H-8083-25, FAA-P-8740-66, POH/AFM]

V. Instrument Approach and Landing with an Inoperative Engine (Simulated)

1. Promptly recognize an engine failure and maintain positive airplane control.

2. Set the engine controls, reduce drag, identify and verify the inoperative engine, and simulate feathering of the propeller on the inoperative engine. (Evaluator should then establish zero thrust on the inoperative engine.)

3. Use flight controls in the proper combination as recommended by the manufacturer, or as required to maintain best performance, and trim as required.

4. Follow the manufacturer's recommended emergency procedures and complete the appropriate checklist.

5. Monitor the operating engine and aircraft systems and make adjustments as necessary.

6. Request and follow an actual or a simulated ATC clearance for an instrument approach.

7. Maintain altitude ±100 feet, or minimum sink rate if applicable; airspeed ±10 knots; and selected heading ±10°.

8. Establish a rate of descent that ensures arrival at the minimum descent altitude (MDA) or decision altitude (DA)/decision height (DH) with the airplane in a position from which a descent to a landing on the intended runway can be made, either straight in or circling as appropriate.

9. On final approach segment, maintain vertical (as applicable) and lateral guidance within ¾-scale deflection.

10. Avoid loss of airplane control, or attempted flight contrary to the operating limitations of the airplane.

(continued)

11. Comply with the published criteria for the aircraft approach category if circling.

12. Execute a landing.

13. Complete the appropriate checklist(s).

Risk Management

Be prepared to identify, assess, and mitigate risks associated with:

1. Potential engine failure during approach and landing.

2. Collision hazards (e.g., aircraft, terrain, obstacles, wires, vehicles, vessels, persons, and wildlife).

3. Configuring the airplane.

4. Low-altitude maneuvering including stall, spin, or CFIT.

5. Distractions, task prioritization, loss of situational awareness, or disorientation.

6. Performing a go-around/rejected landing with an engine failure.

Note: If you do not hold an Instrument–Airplane Rating, this task is not required.

[PA.X.D, CA.X.D; FAA-H-8083-2, FAA-H-8083-3, FAA-H-8083-15, FAA-H-8083-25, FAA-P-8740-66, POH/AFM]

W. After Landing, Parking, and Securing

1. Park in an appropriate area, considering the safety of nearby persons and property.

2. Complete the appropriate checklist(s).

3. Conduct a postflight inspection and document discrepancies and servicing requirements, if any.

4. Secure the airplane.

Risk Management

Be prepared to identify, assess, and mitigate risks associated with:

1. Activities and distractions.

3. Airport specific security procedures.

4. Disembarking passengers safely on the ramp and monitoring passenger movement while on the ramp.

[PA.XII.A, CA.XI.A; FAA-H-8083-2, FAA-H-8083-3, FAA-H-8083-25, POH/AFM]

Appendix 1

Applicant's Practical Test Checklist

Applicant's Practical Test Checklist

Appointment with Examiner

Examiner's Name: _____

Location for test (airport): _____

Date of test: _____

Start time for test: _____

Examiner's fee: _____

Documents to Bring to the Practical Test

___ *Aircraft Maintenance Records*
Logbook record of airworthiness and inspections for engine, aircraft, propeller, and AD compliance:
- Annual inspection
- 100-hour inspection (if applicable)
- VOR test (if applicable)
- Altimeter, pitot static test
- Transponder test
- ELT inspection and battery
- AD compliance documentation
- Current GPS database (if applicable)

___ *Aircraft Required Documents:*
- Supplemental documents
- Placards
- Airworthiness certificate
- Current aircraft registration
- Radio station license
- Owner's manual (AFM/POH)
- Weight and balance documentation

Personal Documents
___ Government-issued photo identification
___ Pilot certificate
___ Aviation Medical Certificate or BasicMed qualification (when applicable)
___ FAA Knowledge Test results
___ Completed FAA Form 8710-1, Airman Certificate and/or Rating Application, with instructor's signature, or completed IACRA form (a best practice is to have both in case of an IACRA system outage)

Training Documentation

___ Log of ground training meeting FAR requirements*

___ Log of flight training meeting FAR requirements

___ Log of experience requirements meeting FAR requirements

___ Endorsements signed by instructor for practical test eligibility

___ Graduation certificate if test will be conducted based on graduation from a Part 141 approved training provider

___ Log of experience indicating currency for flight (flight review endorsement or current solo endorsement; complex, high-performance, or tailwheel endorsement if applicable)

___ Copy of previous Notice of Disapproval (if the test is a retest)

___ Endorsement for retest (if the test is a retest)

A best practice is to have all of these items tabbed or identified to be able to demonstrate eligibility for the practical test to the examiner. The examiner is required to determine and confirm eligibility prior to beginning the test. If they are unable to determine eligibility or you are missing documentation, they may be unable to begin the test and it may need to be rescheduled.

Equipment and Materials to Bring to the Test

___ View-limiting device

___ Current aeronautical charts (printed or electronic)

___ Flight computer, calculator, and/or plotter

___ Flight plan form and flight logs (printed or electronic)

___ *Chart Supplement*, airport diagrams, or other charting resources

___ Current FAR/AIM

* Note that ground training as logged by an online ground school for the FAA Knowledge Test typically does not meet the requirements for ground training for a certificate or rating. Be sure that you have logged ground training for the practical test and that you have it documented and available for review for the practical test.

Appendix 2

Know Your Aircraft

The following are a number of questions related to the specific aircraft you might be using for training and/or a practical test. They reference specific information that is likely sourced from your particular aircraft's airplane flight manual (AFM) or pilot's operating handbook (POH) and apply to questions that may be asked related to operation of the aircraft under normal or emergency conditions. Some of these are very rote-level questions, but they are designed to ensure you have a base of knowledge that can then be applied to more scenario-based questions that will demonstrate your knowledge at the understanding, application, and correlation levels.

Performance and Limitations

Know the performance and limitations of your aircraft, including:

1. Stall speed in the landing configuration (V_{S0}): _____
2. Minimum control speed critical engine inoperative (V_{MC}): _____
3. Stall speed clean (V_S): _____
4. Rotation speed (V_R): _____
5. Lift-off speed (V_{LOF}): _____
6. Best angle-of-climb speed (V_X): _____
7. Best angle-of-climb single engine speed (V_{XSE}): _____
8. Safe intentional one engine inoperative speed (V_{SSE}): _____
9. Best rate-of-climb speed (V_Y): _____
10. Best rate-of-climb single-engine speed (V_{YSE}): _____
11. Maximum flap extended speed (V_{FE}): _____
12. Maximum landing gear operating speed (V_{LO}) [up]: _____
13. Maximum landing gear operating speed (V_{LO}) [down]: _____
14. Maximum landing gear extended speed (V_{LE}): _____
15. Maximum structural cruising speed (V_{NO}): _____
16. Never exceed speed (V_{NE}): _____
17. Design maneuvering speed at gross weight (V_A): _____
18. Maximum demonstrated crosswind speed: _____
19. Best glide speed: _____
20. Normal takeoff:
    flap setting_____ rotation speed_____ climb-out speed_____

21. Normal landing:
    flap setting_____ approach speed_____
22. Short field takeoff:
    flap setting_____ rotation speed_____ climb-out speed_____
23. Short field landing:
    flap setting_____ approach speed_____
24. Soft field takeoff:
    flap setting_____ rotation speed_____ climb-out speed_____
25. Soft field landing:
    flap setting_____ approach speed_____
26. Single-engine approach speed: _____
27. Kinds of operations the aircraft is approved for: _____
28. Accelerate-stop distance: _____
29. Accelerate-go distance: _____
30. Maximum service ceiling: _____
31. Maximum single-engine service ceiling: _____
32. Maximum weight for which single-engine climb
    is possible: _____

Weight and Balance

1. Maximum ramp weight: _____
2. Maximum takeoff weight: _____
3. Maximum landing weight: _____
4. Maximum zero fuel weight: _____
5. Where is/are the baggage compartment(s) located? _____
6. What is/are the maximum weight allowable in the baggage
   compartment(s)? _____
7. How many people will the aircraft carry safely with a full fuel
   load? _____
8. What happens to the CG as fuel is burned off? _____
9. What category is the aircraft certified under? _____
10. What are the flight load factor limits with flaps up? _____
    flaps down? _____
11. Where is the datum line on the aircraft? _____

Primary Flight Controls and Trim

1. What type of control linkages are used for the various flight controls?

2. What type of trim system(s) is/are installed?

3. Does the aircraft have balancing weights attached to the control surfaces? Where?

4. What procedure should be followed if loss of elevator control occurs?

5. If the trim system is electric, what procedure should be used for a "runaway" trim malfunction?

Wing Flaps

1. What type of wing flaps are used (plain, split, slotted, or Fowler flaps)?

2. How are the flaps extended and retracted?

3. What are the different flap extension settings?

4. Where is the flap motor located?

5. If the flap system is electric and an electrical system failure occurs, is there a manual flap extension/retraction procedure?

Powerplant

1. What is the make and model of the engines?

2. What is the maximum continuous operating power for the engine?

3. How many cylinders does the engine have and how are they arranged?

4. Are the engines normally aspirated or turbocharged?

5. Does the engine use fuel injection or carburetion?

6. What type of ignition system is provided?

7. During the before-takeoff static run-up, what is the normal drop expected when checking the magnetos?

8. During the before-takeoff static run-up, what is the maximum differential between the two magnetos?

9. How is engine cooling accomplished?

10. Where are the intakes for normal induction air located?

11. Does the aircraft have an alternate air induction system? How does it work?

12. Describe the cowl flap system on the aircraft.

13. What are normal climb, cruise, and descent power settings?

14. If both the oil and cylinder head temperature gauges are approaching the caution range, what actions can you take to assist in engine cooling?

Propeller

1. Describe the propellers installed on the aircraft.

2. How does an increase or decrease in oil pressure to the propeller affect propeller blade pitch?

3. How is a propeller feathering check accomplished before takeoff?

4. What mechanical device controls oil pressure to the propeller?

5. If applicable, what function do the springs have in the propeller dome?

6. What is the function of the centrifugal stop pins?

7. What is the minimum RPM for feathering?

8. If applicable, what is the function of the nitrogen cylinder?

9. How is a zero thrust condition achieved?

10. How long does it take for the propeller to feather?

11. Explain the procedure used for a propeller overspeed condition.

12. What power settings are used to obtain a zero thrust condition in this aircraft?

Landing Gear

1. What source of power does the landing gear system use for extension and retraction?

2. What type of circuit protection is provided for the landing gear system?

3. What is the normal length of time for either landing gear retraction or extension?

4. What are the flight deck indications for landing gear position?

5. What conditions will cause the landing gear warning horn to sound?

6. What mechanism is used to cause the gear indicator lights to illuminate when the landing gear has fully extended and locked?

7. How is the landing gear locked in the "down" position?

8. How is the landing gear locked in the "up" position?

(continued)

9. How is inadvertent landing gear retraction prevented on the ground?

10. Where are the landing gear "squat" switches located?

11. What is the procedure to follow when one of the landing gear indicator lights fails to illuminate?

12. What is the procedure to follow if the landing gear transit light remains illuminated?

13. If applicable, where is the hydraulic reservoir for the landing gear system located?

14. If applicable, what would happen to the landing gear if a loss of hydraulic pressure occurred while in flight?

15. What is the procedure for manual landing gear extension?

16. Can the landing gear be retracted manually?

17. What type of shock absorption is provided for the landing gear?

18. How is steering accomplished on the ground?

19. When towing the aircraft on the ground, what is the maximum number of degrees the nosewheel may be turned either side of center?

20. What are the tire pressures for the main landing gear and nose wheel tires?

Fuel

1. How many fuel tanks are there and where are they located?

2. What are the capacities of the fuel tanks, both usable and total?

3. How is the fuel quantity measured and indicated?

4. What is the approved fuel grade for the aircraft?

5. If necessary, what alternate grade of fuel is allowed?

6. When servicing the aircraft to a reduced fuel capacity, how can you determine the correct fuel quantity has been added?

7. If a vapor return system is incorporated into the fuel system, which tank will receive the recovered fuel?

8. How many fuel system drains are there and where are they located?

9. Where are the fuel selectors located and what positions are available for selection?

10. Is the fuel system a gravity-fed or pump-driven system?

11. What type of engine priming system is provided?

12. How many fuel pumps are used in the aircraft fuel system?

13. Are the fuel pumps engine-driven or electrical?

14. Where are the auxiliary fuel pumps located?

15. What are the minimum and maximum fuel pressures and fuel flows?

16. When are the electric auxiliary fuel pumps used?

17. What engine performance may be expected when using the auxiliary fuel pumps?

18. What is the recommended procedure when switching fuel tanks prior to the before-takeoff engine run-up?

19. What is the recommended procedure for fuel management during extended flights?

20. How does the fuel crossfeed system operate?

21. In the event of an engine failure, can all of the onboard fuel be fed to the running engine? If yes, explain how.

22. In the event of an engine-driven fuel pump failure, what procedure should be followed?

Note: Be prepared to draw a diagram of the aircraft's fuel system.

Oil

1. Describe the engine oil system.

2. What type and grade of oil is used in the system?

3. What are the minimum and maximum safe oil capacities?

4. What are the minimum and maximum oil temperatures and pressures?

Hydraulic

1. Which of the aircraft's equipment would be considered hydraulic?

2. Do the brakes and landing gear share the same hydraulic system?

3. Give a brief description of the brake system.

4. Are the pilot's brakes totally independent of the copilot's brakes?

5. Where are the hydraulic reservoirs located for the brake system?

6. What type of hydraulic fluid should be used for servicing the hydraulic system?

7. How would a loss of hydraulic pressure be indicated in the flight deck?

Electrical

1. What is the electrical system voltage?
2. What voltage is required for starting from the battery?
3. Where is the battery compartment located?
4. Does the aircraft have generators or alternators?
5. What is the rated amperage of the generators or alternators?
6. Does the aircraft have an APU receptacle and if so, where is it located?
7. How is a high or low voltage condition indicated in the flight deck?
8. How is a generator or alternator failure detected?
9. Does the aircraft have any over-voltage protection?
10. What equipment on the aircraft draws the most electrical current?
11. Are there any limitations on the amount of time the starter can be engaged?
12. What is the procedure for resetting a circuit breaker?
13. If the battery and alternator master switches are switched off, will the engines continue to run?
14. In the event of an alternator failure on one engine, will the remaining alternator be capable of powering any or all loads placed on the electrical system?

Avionics

1. What type of autopilot system is installed?
2. What is the procedure for testing the autopilot prior to takeoff?
3. What aircraft system failures will cause the autopilot to operate erratically?
4. In the event of an autopilot malfunction, what are the different methods the autopilot can be disabled?
5. Is it possible to overpower the autopilot?
6. Can the autopilot be used in the event of a single-engine emergency?
7. Give a brief description of the avionics installed in the aircraft.
8. Describe the location and function of each antenna on the aircraft.

Pitot-Static

1. Which instruments are connected to the pitot-static system?
2. Where are the static port(s) and pitot head(s) on the aircraft?
3. Is there ice protection available for the pitot-static system?
4. Does the aircraft have an alternate-static source?
5. What is the location of the source for alternate-static air?
6. How is the alternate static source activated?
7. Are there any water drains for the static system?

Vacuum/Pressure

1. Which flight instruments are connected to the vacuum/pressure system?
2. How many pumps are used in the vacuum/pressure system?
3. Are the vacuum/pressure pumps engine-driven or electrically driven?
4. What is the required vacuum or pressure for normal instrument operation?
5. How is a vacuum/pressure pump failure indicated?
6. In the event of a vacuum/pressure pump failure (internal failure, engine failure), is manual selection of the operative pump required?
7. During engine-out flight, will the remaining vacuum/pressure pump provide enough suction for the operation of all systems (instruments, deice, etc.)?

Environmental

1. What type of cabin heating system is the aircraft equipped with?
2. Where is the heater located?
3. How is cabin temperature controlled?
4. If there is a combustion heater, what is the fuel source, and how much fuel is used per hour?
5. What are the indications of a heater overheating?
6. Where are the external air inlets for the cabin air/heating system located?
7. Where are the cabin air/heat vents located inside the cabin?

(continued)

8. How is fuel prevented from flowing to a combustion heater that is not being used?

9. If applicable, how would you inspect and test the oxygen system prior to flight?

10. If applicable, what type of information should you brief your passengers on concerning use of the oxygen masks?

11. If applicable, briefly describe how the cabin is pressurized.

Deicing and Anti-Icing

1. Is the aircraft approved for flight in icing conditions?

2. If applicable, what type of anti-ice system is installed on the propellers?

3. If the aircraft is not equipped with propeller deice, what procedures should be followed to prevent ice from forming on the propellers?

4. What type of deice or anti-ice is provided for the leading edges of the aircraft?

5. What is the source of power for the deice or anti-ice system?

6. Is there a deice or anti-ice system for the windshield?

7. Is there any protection from induction-air icing?

Emergency Procedures

Note: Certain immediate action items (such as the response to an engine failure in a critical phase of flight), should be committed to memory. After they are accomplished, and as work load permits, the pilot should verify the action taken with a printed checklist.

1. Engine failure during takeoff prior to rotation

2. Engine failure during takeoff, after rotation

3. Engine failure during climb

4. Engine failure en route

5. Feathering propeller

6. Unfeathering propeller

7. Inflight engine restart

8. Propeller overspeed

9. Securing inoperative engine

10. Fuel management during single-engine operation

11. Single-engine landing

12. Single-engine go-around
13. Landing gear unsafe warning
14. Manual extension of landing gear
15. Gear-up emergency landing
16. Electrical system failures
17. Engine fire on the ground
18. Engine fire in flight
19. Electrical fire on the ground
20. Electrical fire in flight
21. Combustion heater overheat
22. Emergency descent
23. Spin recovery
24. Unlatched door in flight (main and baggage)

Normal Procedures

Note: Be thoroughly familiar with the following normal operating procedures:

1. Preflight inspection
2. Before starting
3. Normal starting
4. Cold engine start
5. Flooded engine start
6. Using external power for start
7. After start and taxi
8. Before takeoff
9. Normal takeoff
10. Short-field takeoff
11. Soft-field takeoff
12. Crosswind takeoff
13. Climb checklist
14. Cruise checklist
15. Engine leaning procedure
16. Descent checklist

(continued)

17. Before landing checklist
18. Normal landing
19. Short-field landing
20. Soft-field landing
21. Crosswind landing
22. Go-around
23. After landing
24. Shutdown

Appendix 3

Operations of Aircraft
Without/With an MEL

Operations of Aircraft *Without* a Minimum Equipment List (MEL)

[14 CFR 91.213, drs.faa.gov]

During the preflight inspection, the pilot discovers inoperative instruments or equipment.

DECISION SEQUENCE:

1. Are the inoperative instruments or equipment part of the VFR-day type certification?

These are the instruments and equipment prescribed in the applicable airworthiness regulations under which the aircraft was type-certificated (14 CFR Part 23 for newer aircraft and CAR Part 3 for much older aircraft).

Note: Referencing the aircraft certification regulations to determine if instruments and equipment are required can be a complex task. In general, the instruments and equipment required by the aircraft certification regulations can be found in the aircraft's Equipment List and Type Certificate Data Sheet (TCDS).

If YES, the aircraft is not airworthy, and maintenance is required before you can fly.

If NO, go to the next step.

[14 CFR 91.213(d)(2)(i)]

2. Are the inoperative instruments or equipment listed as "Required" on the aircraft's equipment list, or on the kinds of operations equipment list (KOEL) for the kind of flight operation being conducted?

Note: Many newer aircraft have a kinds of operations equipment list (KOEL), which refers to the kinds of operations (VFR day, VFR night, IFR day, IFR night, icing) in which the aircraft can operate. The equipment list and KOEL are located in the AFM.

If YES, the aircraft is not airworthy, and maintenance is required before you can fly.

If NO, go to the next step.

[14 CFR 91.213 (d)(2)(ii)]

3. **Are the inoperative instruments or equipment required by 14 CFR §91.205, 91.207, or any other rule of 14 CFR Part 91 for the specific kind of flight operation being conducted?**

   Note: Other required equipment regulations include §91.205 (VFR day, VFR night, IFR); §91.207 (ELTs); §91.209 (aircraft lights); and §91.215 (ATC transponders).

   If YES, the aircraft is not airworthy, and maintenance is required before you can fly.

   If NO, go to the next step.

   [14 CFR 91.213(d)(2)(iii)]

4. **Are the inoperative instruments or equipment required to be operational by an airworthiness directive (AD)? Check the aircraft maintenance logs and/or consult with a maintenance technician to determine AD compliance.**

   If YES, the aircraft is not airworthy, and maintenance is required before you can fly.

   If NO, go to the next step.

   [14 CFR 91.213(d)(2)(iv)]

5. **At this point, the inoperative instruments or equipment must be:**

   REMOVED from the aircraft, the flight deck control placarded, and the maintenance record (logbook) updated in accordance with 14 CFR §43.9. [14 CFR 91.213(d)(3)(i)]

   OR

   DEACTIVATED and PLACARDED "Inoperative." If deactivation of the inoperative instrument or equipment involves maintenance, it must be accomplished and recorded in accordance with 14 CFR Part 43. [14 CFR 91.213(d)(3)(ii)]

6. **Finally, a determination is made by a certificated and appropriately rated pilot or mechanic that the inoperative instrument or equipment does not constitute a hazard to the aircraft for the anticipated conditions of the flight (e.g., day VFR, night VFR, etc.).**

Operations of Aircraft *With* a Minimum Equipment List (MEL)

[14 CFR 91.213, drs.faa.gov]

During the preflight inspection, the pilot discovers inoperative instruments or equipment.

DECISION SEQUENCE:

1. Is the inoperative equipment not included in the MEL, but required by the type certification, AD, or other special conditions?

If **YES**, the aircraft is not airworthy, and maintenance is required before flight.

If **NO**, go to the next step.

2. The pilot performs or has a qualified person perform the appropriate "O" or "M" deactivation or removal procedure.

Note: Two categories of maintenance procedures:

"O" Operations procedures—can be performed by pilot; must be accomplished before or during operation with listed item of equipment inoperative.

"M" Maintenance procedures—must be done by maintenance personnel and be accomplished before beginning operation with the listed item of equipment inoperative.

3. The pilot or maintenance personnel placards the inoperative equipment and updates the maintenance record (logbook).

4. The pilot confirms that the inoperative equipment does not present hazards to the conditions of flight.

Appendix 4

Light Twin Takeoff Control and Performance Briefing

Light Twin Takeoff Control and Performance Briefing

Density altitude = _____

Runway length = _____

Takeoff weight = _____

Takeoff distance = _____

Accelerate-stop distance = _____

Single-engine climb rate = _____

Single-engine service ceiling = _____

V_{MC} = _____

V_R = _____

V_{YSE} = _____

V_Y = _____

If an engine fails below _____ (V_{MC}) or _____ (V_R), I will retard the throttles and abort the takeoff.

If an engine fails after liftoff and the landing gear is down, I will close both throttles an land straight ahead.

If an engine fails after liftoff (at or above V_{XSE}) and the landing gear is retracted, I will follow the POH/AFM procedures to:

- Control (pitch and power for V_{YSE})
- Configure (flaps, gear, and prop)
- Climb (maintain V_{YSE}; zero sideslip)
- Checklist (upon reaching 400 feet AGL)